The Jazz Singer

Wisconsin/Warner Bros. Screenplay Series

The Jazz Singer

Edited with an introduction by

Robert L. Carringer

Published for the Wisconsin Center for Film and Theater Research by
The University of Wisconsin Press

Published 1979

The University of Wisconsin Press
114 North Murray Street
Madison, Wisconsin 53715

The University of Wisconsin Press, Ltd.
1 Gower Street
London WC1E 6HA, England

First printing

Printed in the United States of America

For LC CIP information see the colophon

ISBN 0-299-07660-1 cloth; 0-299-07664-4 paper

Contents

Foreword

The Wisconsin/Warner Bros. Screenplay Series has as its goal the explication of the art of screenwriting during the thirties and forties, the so-called Golden Age of Hollywood. This project is a result of a gift from United Artists to the Wisconsin Center for Film and Theater Research in 1969 consisting of the UA corporate records, the RKO and Monogram film libraries, and, most important, the Warner Film Library. Acquired by United Artists in 1957, during a period when the major studios sold off their films for use on television, the Warner library is by far the richest portion of the gift, containing eight hundred sound features, fifteen hundred short subjects, nineteen thousand still negatives, legal files, and press books, in addition to screenplays for the bulk of the Warner Brothers product from 1930 to 1950. In making this donation, UA created a truly great resource for the study of American film. For the purposes of this project, the company has granted the Center whatever publication rights it holds to the Warner films and has provided the Center the opportunity to advance the cause of film scholarship.

In preparing a critical introduction and annotating the screenplay, the editor of each volume is asked to cover such topics as the development of the screenplay from its source to the final shooting script, differences between the final shooting script and the release print, production information, exploitation and critical reception of the film, its historical importance, its directorial style, and its position within the genre. He is also encouraged to go beyond these guidelines to incorporate supplemental information concerning the studio system of motion picture production.

The script files of the Warner Film Library are vast, containing for most titles the properties on which the films were based, research notes, variant drafts of scripts, press books, and legal records, among other materials. Although the files do not document the conversion to the talkies in the transitional period from 1927 to 1929, we wanted *The Jazz Singer*—the film that triggered the widespread adoption of sound on the part of the industry—to launch the project. Therefore, we turned to the University of Illinois, which had acquired a copy of the shooting script, and to Robert Carringer, who not only was instrumental in building the university's holdings relating to the literature of the cinema but also is the curator of the Samson Raphaelson collection. The print of the film he studied for this volume was the most authoritative one available for reference purposes.

Our thanks to the University of Illinois for providing us with the script and particularly to Samson Raphaelson for his many helpful suggestions.

In the process of preparing this screenplay for publication, typographical errors were corrected, punctuation and capitalization were modernized, and the format was redesigned to facilitate readability. The photographs, except for those credited to other sources, are frame enlargements taken from a 35-mm print of the film provided by United Artists.

Tino Balio
General Editor

Acknowledgments

I owe a special debt of gratitude to the following for their generous assistance in the preparation of this work: Samson Raphaelson, who gave me much valuable information and material; Barry Sabath, who was my research assistant; Tony Slide, who helped me find answers to several problematic questions; John Mullin, who provided historical information on the coming of sound; and Katherine Orloff of Warner Brothers Publicity, who arranged for me to have access to a print of the 1952 *Jazz Singer* film. I am also grateful to the following individuals and institutions for their kind services: Sam Gill, Margaret Herrick Library, Academy of Motion Picture Arts and Sciences; Marshall Deutelbaum, International Museum of Photography, George Eastman House; Steven P. Hill and Edwin Jahiel, Unit for Cinema Studies, and Maynard Brichford, University Archives, University of Illinois at Urbana-Champaign; Paul Myers, Theatre Collection, Library of the Performing Arts at Lincoln Center, New York Public Library; Charles Silver and Emily Sieger, Film Study Center, and Mary Corliss, Film Stills Archive, Museum of Modern Art; Bob Gitt, UCLA Film Archive; Robert Knutson, Cinema Library, University of Southern California; and Tino Balio, Wisconsin Center for Film and Theater Research, University of Wisconsin–Madison. I also acknowledge with deep appreciation the financial assistance provided by the Research Board, Graduate College, University of Illinois at Urbana-Champaign.

R.L.C.

"—he belongs to the whole world now."

Introduction: *History of a Popular Culture Classic*

Robert L. Carringer

The original inspiration for the jazz singer story was an appearance by Al Jolson in Champaign, Illinois, on April 25, 1917. The performance was *Robinson Crusoe, Jr.*, a popular Jolson musical in which he played three roles, including that of Friday. In the audience that evening was Samson Raphaelson, then an undergraduate at the University of Illinois. Raphaelson later recalled of the experience:

I shall never forget the first five minutes of Jolson—his velocity, the amazing fluidity with which he shifted from a tremendous absorption in his audience to a tremendous absorption in his song. I still remember the song, "Where the Black-Eyed Susans Grow." When he finished, I turned to the girl beside me, dazed with memories of my childhood on the East Side. . . . "My God, this isn't a jazz singer. This is a cantor!"

This grotesque figure in blackface, kneeling at the end of a runway which projected him into the heart of his audience, flinging out his white-gloved hands, was embracing that audience with a prayer—an evangelical moan—a tortured, imperious call that hurtled through the house like a swift electrical lariat with a twist that swept the audience right to the edge of that runway. The words didn't matter, the melody didn't matter. It was the emotion—the emotion of a cantor.[1]

Several years later, Raphaelson embarked on his professional literary career with a series of short stories that were published in popular magazines. One of these, "The Day of Atonement," in

1. *American Hebrew*, October 14, 1927, p. 812.

Everybody's Magazine, January 1922 (reprinted on pages 147–67), told the story of a young Jew from the Lower East Side, Jakie Rabinowitz, who forsakes the ways of his fathers to pursue a show business career under the name Jack Robin. Jolson was the model for the character Jack Robin. Like his fictional surrogate, he was descended from several generations of cantors, including a stern, rabbinical father who expected him to follow in his footsteps and who was said to be adamantly opposed to his son's secular musical career; he ran away from home to pursue that career and got his first big show business break in San Francisco; and he fell in love with a *shiksa*, to the great dismay of his orthodox parents.

According to one report, Jolson read "The Day of Atonement" shortly after it was published, was struck by the parallels to his own life, and became intrigued with the possibility of appearing in a film version of it. He first broached the idea to D. W. Griffith through an intermediary, Anthony Paul Kelly, author of the scenario of *Way Down East*, but Griffith declined because of the story's "racial themes." Jolson then sent Kelly on the rounds of the studios, but though they were all interested in Jolson, no one was interested in a Jewish story.[2] In any case, Raphaelson recalls that when he and Jolson were first introduced in a nightclub a few months later, Jolson had already read the story and he expressed interest in having it made into a stage vehicle for him. But when the author saw that what Jolson wanted was another hammed-up musical revue like *Robinson Crusoe, Jr.*, he decided to stick by his serious intentions for the material and he rewrote it as a play. This work (at this stage called "Prayboy") he sold in May 1925 to Broadway producer Al Lewis, who used it as a vehicle to launch George Jessel, up until then a comedian in vaudeville and musical revues, on a career as a dramatic actor. Lewis took over the direction himself, and with the assistance of his partner Max Gordon and their mentor, the great Broadway impresario Sam Harris, guided the play, now titled *The Jazz Singer*, through successful tryouts in Stamford, Asbury Park, and Long Branch over the

2. Herbert G. Goldman, *The Jolson Journal* (International Al Jolson Society), no. 51 (1978), pp. 7–8.

summer and into a smooth opening at the Fulton theater on West Forty-sixth Street on September 14.

The reviews were surprisingly restrained, in view of the play's subject matter. The *Post's* was the most favorable; it began by correctly anticipating the reactions of some of its rivals and made a gallant effort to counter them: "If you are told that *The Jazz Singer* is a tale of a Jewish boy, last of a long line of cantors, who abandons his home by the synagogue to become a knee-sore mammy shouter, falls in love with a high-born prima donna and then, with his starry opening an hour away, renounces the stage to return to Orchard Street and chant his prayers—if you are told these things you may snort, 'Hokum!' and stay away. But if you are informed that this play is literate and interesting, its buncombe obscured by careful construction and sympathetic treatment, its acting genuine—these things will, it is hoped, enroll you among *The Jazz Singer's* patrons."³ More typical was the view of the *Times*: "The play is a shrewd and well-planned excursion into the theatre, concerned with a theme of obvious appeal, and assuredly so written that even the slowest of wits can understand it. *The Jazz Singer* takes no chances with its audiences; it strives always to be successful. The distinct discernibility of the effort probably will be an unimportant factor in the play's career."⁴ At the other end of the spectrum of opinion were the *American*, which called *The Jazz Singer* a "garish and tawdry Hebrew play" presented with "ludicrous and maudlin pomposity," and the *Telegram*, which pronounced it "an illiterate comedy drama, steeped in woe and sentiment." On one thing, however, the reviewers generally agreed: *The Jazz Singer* would find a sure and steady audience. As it turned out, it was the size of that audience that caused the greatest surprise. Because of the limited appeal of the theme, the backers expected *The Jazz Singer* to have a modest but solid run of about three months. All went as expected during the first weeks, but then after the Jewish holidays business picked up and gained steadily over the following weeks and held solid even after a move

3. *New York Post*, September 15, 1925.
4. *New York Times*, September 15, 1925.

to another theater (the Cort) early in November. According to trade reports, the unprecedented volume of business was largely due to a massive promotional campaign aimed mainly at the Jewish community, and the houses were said to be about 90 per cent Jewish. Jessel himself gave the cause a major boost through an aggressive personal appearance effort and regular publicity interviews carefully tied in with the content of the play:

My business ventures had failed and I had not found faith. The story of *The Jazz Singer* came to me at an eleventh hour. I was singing in an all-night cafe at the time and theatricals appealed to me.

When the curtain fell on the opening night on September 14, 1925, I made a speech in which I told the audience that I hoped I would be able to find faith in real life as I found it in the character I was playing on the stage. My hope and wish were realized, for I soon became convinced that I could not continue to live as I had and give a sincere performance. I had found faith and I turned about face and became a new George Jessel. I remarried my wife, from whom I had been separated, changed my mode of living, and became in reality the man I am portraying on the stage.[5]

Business continued to hold throughout the winter and into the spring, and *The Jazz Singer* could probably have gone on indefinitely. But Jessel had a Hollywood commitment and, to accommodate his schedule, the New York run was ended on June 5, after thirty-eight weeks, and the road tour postponed.

Production Plans

Undoubtedly it was this surprise box-office success that sparked Warner Brothers' interest in a property of such purportedly limited appeal as *The Jazz Singer*. That is what had sold them on Jessel, who had signed an exclusive three-year picture contract with Warners back in April. Immediately after the closing of the play, Jessel left for Hollywood to begin work on his first film, *Private Izzy Murphy*, one in a wave of Irish-Jewish boy-meets-girl romances being turned out at the time in the wake of the enormous success of the play *Abie's Irish Rose* on Broadway. On June 4, the day before the play closed, Warners bought the picture rights to *The Jazz Singer* for fifty thousand dollars. Ernst Lubitsch, Warn-

5. *New York American*, February 14, 1926.

ers' leading director at the time, had initiated the transaction in a wire of May 20, and he was originally intended to direct the picture. Though Lubitsch's specialty since coming to America had been sophisticated comedy, by this time the Warners were actively encouraging him to branch off into new subject areas and especially to undertake specifically American subjects. (Lubitsch later told Raphaelson he had been greatly interested in filming *The Jazz Singer*.)

To protect the upcoming road tour of the play, the contract stipulated that the film could not be released until May 1, 1927. There were reports early in the summer that production might be imminent (according to one account, the Warners were considering the possibility of shooting the film in the East in the fall, and, according to another, they were thinking of holding Jessel over after *Private Izzy Murphy* and making it in Hollywood). Finally it was decided that production would be postponed until Jessel's return to Hollywood the following spring after touring with the play. Jessel returned to New York in August and opened on the road in Boston on Labor Day. Business was unusually good in the four-week Boston engagement, and it continued to hold up extremely well throughout the winter, especially in places like Chicago, Milwaukee, St. Louis, and Philadelphia. The tour finally ended the following spring with what *Variety* called a "surprise booking"—a two-week rerun at the mammoth Century theater in New York beginning April 18.

During Jessel's absence, however, the situation in Hollywood had greatly changed. Lubitsch had left Warner Brothers the previous August, first to make *The Student Prince* at MGM and then to embark on his long and successful reign as top director at Paramount. That same month, Warner Brothers had introduced its new Vitaphone sound-on-disc process with a special program that opened at the Warners theater in New York on Friday, August 6. The program consisted of eight shorts—a spoken welcome by Will Hays, the overture to *Tannhäuser* played by the New York Philharmonic, several other vocal and instrumental excerpts from classical music, vaudeville guitarist Roy Smeck doing a novelty act—and John Barrymore in a feature with synchronized music and sound effects, *Don Juan*. In retrospect, it is this date, and not the date *The Jazz Singer* premiered, that marks the opening of the sound era. There had been efforts from the beginning to add sound to pictures, but sound was generally considered an expensive novelty in Hollywood because of the high cost of reequipping both the studios and the theaters. Warner Brothers had originally approached Vitaphone cautiously as a process that would bring vaudeville and other stage talent to movie audiences and provide orchestral accompaniment for their features. The Vitaphone venture was one step in a major plan of expansion that had been under way at Warner Brothers for some time, and its development was to be the principal factor in catapulting Warners into the ranks of the major studios by the early 1930s. The response to the *Don Juan* program was sufficiently enthusiastic to encourage the Warners to move ahead with their plans to develop Vitaphone. A second Vitaphone program was premiered in New York early in October, this one with an all-vaudeville shorts prologue (which included both Jessel and Jolson in separate shorts) and a comedy feature, *The Better 'Ole,* with Sydney Chaplin; a third, early in February, had a prologue that mixed popular and operatic music, followed by another John Barrymore romance, *When a Man Loves,* adapted from L'Abbé Prévost's novel *Manon Lescaut.* Production of these early Vitaphone programs had been centered in the East, but early in 1927 construction began on a major new studio complex for Vitaphone productions on the thirteen-acre Warner Brothers lot on Sunset Boulevard in Hollywood. By the time Jessel returned to Hollywood, the first of these new stages was ready to go into operation.

Jolson Replaces Jessel

On February 19, 1927, *Moving Picture World* reported that Jessel would start work on the *Jazz Singer* film on May 1. The same news item indicated that part of the original cast of the play would appear with Jessel in the film, and also that Warners was engaged in a search for yet another vehicle for Jessel, which would go into production on June 15, after completion of *The Jazz Singer.* Three months later, with Jessel already in Hollywood and shooting on the film about to begin, Jessel was replaced by Jolson.

Explanations of this surprise turn of events have proliferated over the years. One story in circulation at the time was that Jessel balked when he found that Jack Warner was going to cast non-Jewish performers, Warner Oland and Eugenie Besserer, as the parents. Another story (the one told most often) was that Jessel and the Warners couldn't get together on the money. Though the amounts and parties involved differ from telling to telling, according to most sources (including parties close to the situation but not directly involved, such as Eddie Cantor and Al Lewis) the general situation seems to have developed as follows: Jessel's pre-Vitaphone contract with Warners was conceived in terms of silent pictures. When Jessel learned that *The Jazz Singer* was to be shot in Vitaphone, he wanted a new deal. The Warners resented this, refused to meet his terms, and opened negotiations with Jolson, who eventually signed for the role late in May.

It would help if we knew more about what the Warners were doing behind the scenes at this time. In any case, it is hard to see how the turn of events could have left them anything but elated. The short-term gamble on mixed Vitaphone programs had paid off, but the bigger gamble—full-length features with their own sound performances—had yet to be taken. A major investment had been made to equip the West Coast operation for the production of Vitaphone features; the studio roster was being filled out with talent to make them—Alan Crosland, for instance, who had directed *Don Juan*, and Warner Oland, who had appeared in it, had both recently been signed to long-term contracts; and the company now also had its own theaters and was rapidly equipping a huge number of them with Vitaphone. In the May 21 issue of *Moving Picture World*, in an article announcing the casting of Otto Lederer as Yudelson, the upcoming *Jazz Singer* is described as an "Extended Run Production"—that is, an expensive prestige item the studio was prepared to go all out on. Jessel was a vaudeville comedian and master of ceremonies with one successful play and one modestly successful film to his credit. Jolson was a superstar. The following week, *Moving Picture World* (issue of May 28), announced *The Jazz Singer* as the "first Vitaphone production to be made by Warners on the coast" (p. 253) and published several other news items on *The Jazz Singer*. Their juxtaposition is very intriguing. One of them, announcing the signing of Cantor Rosenblatt for a musical performance in the film, refers to *The Jazz Singer* as the "first motion picture made with Vitaphone sequences," and says this event "marks an epoch in motion picture production" (p. 273). Another article (p. 253) reveals Sam Warner's arrival in Hollywood to "take charge of the Vitaphone interests of Warner Brothers" and to "inaugurate the production of Vitaphone pictures in an annex to the original studios, erected especially for this purpose." (Sam was the brother who had pushed the Vitaphone venture from the first; persistent reports also indicate he was the one who opened negotiations with Jolson, through an intermediary.) His arrival is said to have given rise to a report "that there may be some change in the Vitaphone policy in order to meet the competition of many other talking devices which have flooded the market, particularly since the Vitaphone made its debut." In the "first Vitaphone production" article on the same page is a statement that shooting on *The Jazz Singer* would begin in about a week, when its star, George Jessel, was due to arrive from the East. On the facing page is the following item: "Warner Bros. announce the acquisition of Al Jolson, who will make his debut on the screen in the title role of *The Jazz Singer*, the drama which broke all records in New York and on tour the past two years. Jolson is now in Hollywood and starts making *The Jazz Singer* immediately."

Jolson had signed with Warner Brothers on May 26. His contract stipulated that, in addition to starring in the picture, he would record in synchronization for it a total of six songs—"Kol Nidre," "Mammy," "When I Lost You," "Yes, Sir, That's My Baby," "Mighty Lak a Rose," and "An Everything," or any mutually acceptable substitutes. For eight weeks' services, beginning July 11, 1927, he was to receive $75,000 ($25,000 in cash, the balance at $6,250 per week), plus $9,375 per week for any work after eight weeks. Stories have also proliferated over the years about additional arrangements beyond the contract. According to one of these (implied by *Billboard* at the time and later repeated by both Jessel and a Jolson biographer, Michael Freedland), Jolson put some of his own money in the production in order to get the part (the sum reported ranges from $180,000 to—as Jolson said to

Jessel—"about a million dollars"). Another story is that Jolson made what amounted to a percentage deal, taking a certain sum in cash and the balance in Warners stock. (Again, the reported figures vary from a combined total of $75,000 to a combined total of $200,000.) According to one source, the entire arrangement was made contingent on a screen test.

Jolson did take a screen test around the middle of June, and *Moving Picture World* reported on June 18 that the result "exceeded the [Warners'] highest hopes." Jolson then left for an out-of-town engagement. Meanwhile, several exterior scenes in which the main performers were not involved were being shot, but principal photography was held up pending Jolson's return and the arrival of other featured players. The exterior scenes on the Lower East Side and in front of the Shuberts' Winter Garden theater were shot on location in New York by Alan Crosland the latter part of June and the first part of July. (Warner Oland and Otto Lederer went east with him to appear in some of the Lower East Side scenes.) Jolson returned toward the middle of July to begin actual filming. His silent sequences were shot first. The complicated Vitaphone sequences were done mainly in the latter part of August.

Jolson originally recorded, on August 16 and 17, "It All Depends on You" as Jack Robin's homecoming song for his mother, but this sequence was reshot on August 30 with "Blue Skies" substituted—and possibly for the purpose of allowing Jolson to deliver his famous monologue. *Motion Picture News* reported on September 23 that *The Jazz Singer* "was completed this week at the Warner studio in Hollywood after four months of work." After finishing up with his part in the production early in September, Jolson did a one-week stage show at the Metropolitan theater in Los Angeles, rested up for a few days at Arrowhead Springs, traveled to Chicago for the Dempsey-Tunney rematch on September 22, then went on to New York for the premiere. Meanwhile, Jessel had completed work on two Warners silent pictures, *The Great Ginsberg* and *Sailor Izzy Murphy*, and was back in the East touring again with the *Jazz Singer* play. *Variety* reported on October 5 that figures from such places as Newark and the Bronx showed that publicity for the upcoming New York premiere of the film was definitely helping the play. The play continued to do excellent business on the road for a while after the film had opened in New York, but as the film edged out into more and more locations, it gradually forced the play out of business.

Raphaelson's Story and Play

The *Jazz Singer* film opened on October 6, 1927, at the Warners theater in New York. (Ironically, Sam Warner had died in Hollywood the day before, and none of the Warner brothers was present for the opening.) One of the invited guests in the audience that evening was Samson Raphaelson, the author of the original story and the play, who many years later recalled his reactions to the experience:

The picture opened with East Side shots. Then I saw this cantor. They "refined" him, you see. His whiskers were beautifully combed, as if he had been to a beauty parlor. And the mother was made just too spotlessly clean, as though she were demonstrating stoves or refrigerators. The whole damned thing—the dialogue, whatever they had taken from my innocent play was either distorted or broken up. I had a simple, corny, well-felt little melodrama, and they made an ill-felt, silly, maudlin, badly timed thing of it. There was absolutely no talent in the production at all, except the basic talent of the floating camera. The cameraman has always been a tremendous fellow. The sets were good, you know; if they took a shot of the East Side, it was a damned good camera shot and stands up today as a damned good camera shot. That was there—the photography.

Jolson didn't have any comedy dialogue. The man's a terrific comedian—and a lousy actor. He's a non-actor. They gave him "dramatic" scenes—that is, "straight" scenes—terribly written synopsis dialogue—and he didn't try to play them; he just read them. It was embarrassing. A dreadful picture. I've seen very few worse.

. . . They put a lot of songs in that were bad, and badly placed. They didn't develop the relationships so that you could feel the characters. The characters were just indicated—as you would in a synopsis. The corny part was overdone, was done far worse than in the play. At least I had built my characters—they were based on people I knew. My situations had coincidence in them; but my characters were real, they were out of my childhood. There were no characters in the movie. Just a line here and a line there, and boom, into a phony cafe background, the most routine kind of backstage-musical sort of stuff. Then Jolson would sing a song, and the songs were ill-chosen, except for one that I dimly remember he sang in his home with his mother, illustrating to her the kind of stuff he sings. The big moment was ridiculous—when he's rehearsing his big show, and he hears his father is dying, and his mother comes to beg him to replace his father on the eve of the Day of Atonement, and it's dress rehearsal afternoon and as his mother is begging him, he's suddenly told, "Go on for your number," and he has to leave his mother behind as he goes on for his number.

Now, that situation basically was from my play, but in my play the song I had him sing was—Lord Almighty, the one thing that I wouldn't have him sing was a song about *mother*. There's a limit. . . .

I could see tremendous possibilities, once I heard sound on film. You heard background noises; as you went through the East Side, you heard the street sounds, and so on. I could see a whole new era had come into the theatre. But from this particular picture, you wouldn't have much hope for the possibilities of that era.[6]

Those who know the short story and the play will be able to sympathize with Raphaelson's disappointment with the film. Both of the original versions manage to resist the more luridly melodramatic overtones of their subject matter, and they can be said to achieve a certain measure of dignity and decorum. The story, especially, has strengths that are lacking in the later versions. These derive particularly from its strong undertow of psychological anxiety.

"The Day of Atonement" is the story of youthful initiation into the realities of adult life, and none of the pain of these rites is spared. On his way home from swimming, young Jakie Rabinowitz is taunted in the streets by an Irish boy. He breaks his gang's "code" by trying to shrug it off instead of fighting back and ends up having to fight one of the members of his own gang. After the fight is over and he is lying on the curb with a black eye and a bloody nose, he hurls the Irish boy's racial slur back at a member of his own gang. When the boy announces his resistance to becoming a cantor, he receives a beating from his father. After he goes on the stage, his life continues to be a series of psychological ordeals. He falls in love with a beautiful dancer in the show but is afraid to approach her because she is a *shiksa* from a good Boston family. His performances go from bad to worse. He begins to drink. In

6. Columbia Oral History Transcription.

probably the best passage in the story, Jack describes the peace he feels when he returns home between bookings one summer and visits his father's synagogue:

As he sat on the old familiar wooden bench, clothed in the silk *Talis*—the prayer-shawl which his father had so solemnly presented to him on the occasion of his *Bar Mitzvah*—with good old Yudelson, the cobbler, on one side of him, and stout, hearty, red-bearded Lapinsky, the butcher, on the other, he felt a singular warmth and sweetness. And the voice of his father, still clear and lyric, rising in the intricacies of the familiar old lamenting prayers—prayers which he remembered perfectly, which he would never forget—the dissonant rumble of response from the congregation, the restive shufflings of youngsters—all these were to him blessedly familiar and blissful.

Though "The Day of Atonement" is technically unsophisticated as a story, it is not without some significance for its subject matter. It stands on the threshold of what was to become a major literary genre, the American Jewish novel of assimilation. When we recall that before it there was not much more of importance in the line than Abraham Cahan's sketches and novels and the very early work of Ben Hecht, its achievement seems all the more impressive.

In adapting his story for the stage, Raphaelson shifted the emphasis in the material from Jack's private turmoils to the actual scenes of conflict. Act 1 opens in the Rabinowitz home years after Jack has left. It is the cantor's sixtieth birthday. He is coaching a young alto. He and his wife quarrel over a letter she has received from Jack. Finally Jack himself shows up to celebrate his father's birthday, and the old man throws him out. Act 2 is set at the theater. The show is about to open and some of the routines are being rehearsed. Jack and Mary appear. A subplot is introduced in which one of the backers, an ex-fiancé of Mary's, withdraws his money from the show because he resents her attentions to Jack. Yudelson arrives to tell Jack the old cantor is ill and begs him to come home and sing for Yom Kippur. Unsuccessful, Yudelson leaves. Later, in Jack's dressing room, Jack's mother enters as he is blacking his face. She begs Jack to come home. Drama; pathos. Jack is called away to rehearsal. While he is offstage, in blackface, singing a maudlin song, his mother, left alone in his dressing room, listens, heartbroken, then slowly goes. Act 3 returns to the Rabinowitz home. By the time Jack arrives, the cantor has already been taken to the hospital. The producer comes and pleads with Jack to return to the show. Then Mary arrives and Jack is made to undergo the full agonies of his indecision. Finally, the doctor telephones that the cantor is dead, and Jack goes to the synagogue to sing in his place.

Like all the versions of *The Jazz Singer*, the play labors under the burden of a portentous theme, that Jack's jazz singing is fundamentally an ancient religious impulse seeking expression in a modern, popular form. Or, as the author himself puts it, in a preface to his published play that (probably consciously) has strong echoes of Walt Whitman:

He who wishes to picture today's America must do it kaleidoscopically; · he must show you a vivid contrast of surfaces, raucous, sentimental, egoistical, vulgar, ineffably busy—surfaces whirling in a dance which sometimes is a dance to Aphrodite and more frequently a dance to Jehovah.

In seeking a symbol of the vital chaos of America's soul, I find no more adequate one than jazz. Here you have the rhythm of frenzy staggering against a symphonic background—a background composed of lewdness, heart's delight, soul-racked madness, monumental boldness, exquisite humility, but principally prayer.

I hear jazz, and I am given a vision of cathedrals and temples collapsing and, silhouetted against the setting sun, a solitary figure, a lost soul, dancing grotesquely on the ruins. . . . Thus do I see the jazz singer.

Jazz is prayer. It is too passionate to be anything else. It is prayer distorted, sick, unconscious of its destination. The singer of jazz is what Matthew Arnold said of the Jew, "lost between two worlds, one dead, the other powerless to be born."[7]

What helps to save the play is what also helps to save the story: restraint and the deliberate underplaying of the more highly melodramatic elements, such as the old man's death, the jazz singing, and the religious pageantry—all of which are made to take place offstage. And again as with the story, the value of the play may be seen more clearly in historical context. Despite a thriving Yiddish theater tradition in America (or perhaps partly

7. Samson Raphaelson, *The Jazz Singer* (New York: Brentano's, 1925), pp. 9–10.

because of it), a native tradition of avowedly Jewish drama was very slow to emerge. The early efforts were usually comedic, such as Aaron Hoffman's *Welcome Stranger* (opened 1920), about a Jewish merchant who settles in a New England village and eventually wins the affections of all his neighbors. (His case is helped along considerably when it is discovered that the worst of the anti-Semites is himself a Jew who is passing as a Gentile.) The most popular Jewish-content play on Broadway in the 1920s, however, was written by a non-Jew. *Abie's Irish Rose*, by Anne Nichols, opened at the Fulton theater on May 23, 1922, played continuously until 1927, and ran up an astonishing total of 2,532 performances. It tells the story of a Jewish boy and an Irish girl who met overseas during the war, married, and now come home to face their parents. Abie introduces his bride, Rosemary Murphy, to his father as Rosie Murphyski. Abie and Rosie are remarried first by a rabbi to please one side of the family, then by a Catholic priest to please the other side. All turns out well in the end, however, when Rose gives birth to twins, a boy who is called Patrick Joseph and a girl who is called Rebecca.

The characters of *Abie's Irish Rose* are a gallery of ethnic stereotypes, from the cherubic, otherworldly priest and the brawny, red-faced, quick-tempered father on the Irish side, to the fretting matriarch, penurious father, and officious rabbi on the Jewish side. The Jewish stereotypes in particular are exploited to the full for low comedy effects:

MRS. COHEN (to Solomon): Vod a vedding! Solomon, you have did yourself proud for vonce.
SOLOMON: Oi! Oi!
MRS. COHEN: Vod's the matter? Iss the expense worrying you already yet?
COHEN (now thoroughly alarmed at Solomon's distress): Mama, he's been doink dod since I came in, after the wedding.
MRS. COHEN: Solomon, heve you god a pain?
SOLOMON: I've god a sometink. I didn't vont, but now I've god it!
MRS. COHEN: That's the way I felt too about my appendix.
SOLOMON: It ain't my appendixes! I vish it vas!

(act 2)

The Jazz Singer was written partly as a response to *Abie's Irish Rose*. It attempts to deal seriously with the same matters that *Abie's Irish*

Rose treats frivolously, and it tries to give a sincere portrait of life as it may actually be lived in a time of crisis for a Jewish family—as a mixture of high tragedy, low comedy, and everyday routine. It also tries to present Jewish customs and lore in a fashion that avoids both the pageantry-spectacle of productions like *The Dybbuk* at one extreme and the vaudevillian buffoonery of *Abie's Irish Rose* on the other. A good example is the opening scene with the cantor and his young pupil, which blends exposition, religious devotion, and comedy:

(Moey is singing.)
CANTOR (stops him): No, no, no! Didn't I tell you how you should sing it? Sing it with a sigh. Do you understand, my child? With a sigh! You are praying to God. Nu, try it again. (Moey tries again, and again is stopped by cantor.) No—do you understand what it means, them words you are singing? What does "Vaanee Sefeelosee" mean?
MOEY: It means, "I, my prayer."
CANTOR: And what means "Lecho Adoshem"?
MOEY: That means, "To you, O God."
CANTOR: Good! And what does it mean, "Ais Rutzon Elohim"?
MOEY: "When you are ready, O God."
CANTOR: That's right. You're a smart boy, Moey. Now what does it mean "Berov Chasdecho Aneni Be-emes Yishecho"?
MOEY (hesitates): I don't know what that means.
CANTOR: Is *that* nice? A smart boy like you what has the most beautiful voice in the choir? You will never learn to sing until you know what the words mean. Now, listen, Moey. This is what it means. "I offer my prayer to you, when you are ready, O God, with your multitudes of benedictions—answer me, O God, with truth, and help me." Sing it again, Moey.

The Film

The reviewer for the *New York Times* observed of the *Jazz Singer* play that it "takes no chances with its audiences." One wonders what he would have said about the film. Where the play was characterized by understatement and restraint, the film is characterized by the opposite. All the emotional valves are turned full open. Mother-love is made the dominant emotion. Sara Rabinowitz is continually displayed in all the familiar tear-jerking poses:

slaving over her hot stove, gazing at her lost son's photograph, weeping in the temple, lighting candles, and suffering in silence, eyes closed, tears streaming down her cheeks. After Jakie leaves, the old cantor goes on alone and plaintively wails the "Kol Nidre." Cantor Rosenblatt appears and sings a eulogy for the dead. There are long, drawn-out tearful scenes in which nothing is spared, as when Sara visits her son backstage and begs him to come home, and later when the prodigal returns at last and, as the camera lingers close, receives his dying father's blessing. True to melodramatic form, Jack himself gets to have it both ways in the end, skipping the opening of his show to sing the "Kol Nidre" but somehow making a hit anyway and appearing at the Winter Garden as a big star at the end. Ironically, Warner Brothers ended up doing what the original author had managed with great effort to avoid, making *The Jazz Singer* into a kind of tragic *Abie's Irish Rose*.

The jazz singer story was most valuable to Warner Brothers for its modern-day plot involving a protagonist who is a performer of popular music. This plot provided a basis for integrating the sound performances, which had been presented separately as prologues in the earlier Vitaphone presentations, with the action of the feature. Beyond this, what is most valuable or significant in the film has not much to do with the dramatic values of the original material.

Besides abandoning itself to sentimentality, the film also changes the overall nature of the story. Both of the original versions end with Jack Robin's going to the synagogue to sing in his father's place. The film ends with Jack's singing to a packed house at the Winter Garden. This ending was not in Alfred A. Cohn's original scenario, and it was undoubtedly added as part of the overall process of transforming the material into a vehicle for Jolson. On the other hand, it was also a logical culmination of a development that was already well under way when Jolson came in. The play has a carefully compressed time scheme: Jack's homecoming, the principal event of the first act, is set on an afternoon in August; all the rest—the backstage business, Mary, the crisis over the show's opening, the Yom Kippur service—takes place on a single day a month later. One of Cohn's principal changes in adapting the material was to add a new beginning with Jack as a boy of thirteen dead set on a show business career and already in open rebellion against his father's wishes. As a result of this change, related changes elsewhere, and the new Jolson ending, the story is transformed from a fable of adjustment (how the new generation finds its place in a cultural tradition) to a more characteristically American fable of success—open revolt against tradition, westward movement, the expenditure of energy, triumph, and the replacement of the values of the old by the values of the new.

These new story values are especially well reflected in the film in such elements as a strikingly energetic opening montage of the Lower East Side and the frenetic scenes of rehearsal that predominate through the middle portions, both of which are in very strong contrast visually to the rather stodgily filmed and edited scenes in the home and the synagogue. This hybridization was eventually to lead to consequences for Warner Brothers that extended well beyond the transitional era of the coming of sound. For if we remove the Jewish elements from the *Jazz Singer* film, what we are left with—the drive to success, the relentless pace of the chorus line in rehearsal, the show-must-go-on motif, the miraculous last-minute leap over fate and circumstances, the resounding triumph at the end—are the main plot elements of one of the most successful genres in the studio's history, the backstage musical of the thirties.

An additional significance of the film has virtually nothing at all to do with the original story. Jolson interpolates a few lines of spoken dialogue between numbers in his first musical sequence. Later he pauses in the middle of a number he is singing for his mother to tell her what he is going to do for her if the show is a success. (Her mumbled reactions are heard. Shortly after, when the cantor arrives on the scene, we also hear his enraged "Stop!") According to legend, the irrepressible Jolson started blurting out lines without warning on the set and the Warners were highly pleased with the results. On the other hand, a feature article on Vitaphone in *Motion Picture News* of July 8, 1927, indicates that the Warners were already discussing the use of dialogue experimentally in *The Jazz Singer* well before the film went into production (see pages 175–79). It would have been a logical and characteristic next step in their careful Vitaphone strategy—a move sufficiently bold to evoke strong audience response one way or the other, but advanced cautiously enough so that they could cut their losses if need be. In any case, *The Jazz Singer* is a special historical landmark as the first Hollywood feature film in which spoken dialogue was used as part of the dramatic action.

Remakes

The original stars of the two productions continued to be identified with *The Jazz Singer* for many years. When Warner Brothers was planning a tenth-anniversary remake of the *Jazz Singer* film in 1936, it wanted Jolson once again for the title role, along with Ruby Keeler in the Mary Dale part and Jean Hersholt or Lionel Barrymore as the cantor. (*The Song and Dance Man* and later *Bowery to Broadway* were used as working titles to disguise the nature of this project.) Milton Krims was assigned to do a new story, musical arrangements were made, and a tentative starting date of October 15 was set, but late in the year the venture was abandoned.

On Monday, August 10, 1936, Jolson starred in a radio version of the story broadcast on WABC, New York. Karen Morley appeared as Mary Dale, and Sara Rabinowitz was portrayed by veteran Yiddish mama Vera Gordon. The reviewer for the *New York Daily News* felt that the "old play has stood the test of time remarkably well," and said that this production "must go down in the books as one of the most effective . . . in WABC's Radio Theatre." Jolson did a second radio version of *The Jazz Singer* on June 2, 1947, in the wake of the success of *The Jolson Story*. Jessel was trying as late as 1939 to mount a revival of the play with himself in the original role, but like several previous efforts, this one never materialized. One reason is clear. By 1939 Jessel was already in his forties. (Jolson was well into his fifties.) It is no surprise, then, that when another film remake was being contemplated a few years later, Warner Brothers would look for new faces.

On January 30, 1945, *Daily Variety* reported that Warner Brothers was undertaking a "modernized" version of *The Jazz Singer*.

Studio records indicate that Paul Muni was under consideration for the lead role at this time. Several months later, on September 10, 1945, *Hollywood Reporter* carried a follow-up story indicating that Dane Clark would play the lead in this production. An item in the *Reporter* the next day said that Michael Curtiz would direct and that the role of Mary Dale would go to Eleanor Parker. Later reports indicated that Alex Gottlieb would produce and that Leo Robin and Arthur Schwartz had been assigned to do the music.

Several factors probably influenced the studio's interest in such a remake at this time. For one, musical biography was undergoing a spectacular resurgence. Columbia released *A Song to Remember* (with Paul Muni) in March 1945; Warners released *Rhapsody in Blue* in June; and *The Jolson Story* was in preparation at Columbia. For another, the cycle of pictures dealing with the problems of soldiers returning to civilian life was about to go into full swing. Dane Clark had been very popular in the role of bantam tough-guy in several Warner Brothers war pictures, and he had recently appeared (both times with Eleanor Parker) in two of the early readjustment pictures, *The Very Thought of You* and *Pride of the Marines*. The jazz singer story was updated to wartime for this remake, so it is probably safe to assume that this version was being planned as an entry in the readjustment cycle (*Abie's Irish Rose* was undergoing a similar transformation at the time for a remake for United Artists in 1946) and as a vehicle to launch Clark into starring roles. Finally, the plight of the Jews in Europe had created a more favorable climate in Hollywood for Jewish subjects generally, as *Crossfire* and *Gentleman's Agreement* were shortly to attest. On November 28, 1945, however, *Variety* announced that the *Jazz Singer* remake had been shelved, reportedly out of concern that *The Jolson Story* was covering a good deal of the same ground. In the same story, John Garfield is mentioned as the intended lead, perhaps a sign that the studio had cooled on its original plans for Clark.

In any case, the wartime premise was revived once again in 1952, when Curtiz completed a Warner Brothers remake of *The Jazz Singer*, with Danny Thomas as a soldier who returns home from the war in Korea to face a choice between the life of a cantor and a career as a singer. The Mary Dale part was originally to have been played by Doris Day, who had been teamed successfully with Thomas the year before in *I'll See You in My Dreams*, a musical biography of songwriter Gus Kahn also directed by Curtiz, but she was replaced at the last minute by singer Peggy Lee. Veteran character actor Eduard Franz was cast as the cantor. Mildred Dunnock was the understanding mother torn between her love for father and son, a role reminiscent of the one she had recently played to perfection in the stage and film versions of *Death of a Salesman*. The film was shot in Hollywood during August and September 1952 and was premiered in Miami on New Year's Eve. It also had a well-publicized benefit opening in New York on January 13, 1953. Not surprisingly, it did record business in wintertime Miami. But elsewhere the results were disappointing. It is not hard to see why. Despite Technicolor, high production values, Peggy Lee's singing, a superb performance by Mildred Dunnock, impressive liturgical scenes, and generally slick direction, the *Jazz Singer* remake is a surprisingly listless and enervated work. Much of the dialogue is insipid; the plot is meandering ("overlong with too many climaxes," as the *Variety* reviewer put it); and Danny Thomas seems uncomfortable in the part. But there is also a more fundamental flaw.

The 1952 *Jazz Singer* is set not in the Lower East Side ghetto but in a prosperous neighborhood of North Philadelphia. Its well-to-do congregation worships in a magnificent edifice (Sinai Temple in Los Angeles was the location actually used) and supports its rabbi in a style befitting a business executive or college president. Though the hero of the story is still in love with a singer, the question of intermarriage has disappeared as an issue. (After an objection was made to studio executives by an influential rabbi that the problem of intermarriage had no place in the picture, Peggy Lee dubbed a throwaway line to establish that she is Jewish—a remark to the mother that she hasn't attended a Seder since she left home.) Yudelson of the early versions, a Yiddish comic stereotype but also chairman of the congregation and a facilitator, is updated in 1952 to everybody's "Uncle Louie," a feckless but lovable figure whose comic tag is his inability to stick with anything for very long.

The original jazz singer story drew its principal energies from the elemental conflicts underlying a precise historical moment for the first-generation Jew in America—sacred versus profane, Jew versus Gentile, ascetic versus libertine, deprivation versus economic promise, immobility versus displacement, love for a *shiksa* versus a girl of one's own kind. By the 1950s, however, the American Jew had by and large been assimilated into the overall texture of American life. As a consequence, updating the story tended to remove the basis for most of the original terms of conflict. (What conflicts did remain, moreover, tended to be glossed over or elided—as with the case of intermarriage.) Nowhere is the change more evident or telling than in the role of the old cantor. In the 1920s versions he was steadfast and unwavering to the end, a reflection of the strength and authority of the cultural heritage he stood for. In the 1950s version, on the other hand, he is made a figure of cultural bifurcation. His son is to assume his place, he says, not only because they come from a long line of cantors but also because they have lived together in the same house and attended the "same university." Although he banishes his son and reads the prayer for the dead over him, he can also correctly recite the full text of an abominable radio commercial the son recorded. When at last he is on what everyone thinks is his deathbed, he relents, accepts the path his son has chosen, and asks his son to forgive *him*. He makes a surprise recovery, however, and in a final gesture of capitulation is seen seated beside his wife in the audience of a New York show, beaming along with her as his son performs a popular song onstage. A key scene of both the play and the 1927 film showed Jack returning home on his father's sixtieth birthday, bringing him a gift of a prayer shawl. In the 1952 version, it is the mother's birthday instead, and the gift, which apparently comes by messenger, is a three-quarter-length mink coat. Though the 1952 *Jazz Singer* retains the original story situation, it is little more than an outer shell enclosing material whose fundamental terms are not conflict but rather affluence and adjustment.

The Jazz Singer was revived once again when Jerry Lewis played the part in the Ford "Startime" series on NBC television on October 13, 1959. Anna Maria Alberghetti was cast in the Mary Dale part, Molly Picon was the mother, and Eduard Franz recreated his 1952 role as cantor. The reviewer for the *New York Times* felt that

Lewis's performance "had the virtue of simplicity and direction," and that "he survived last night's interesting experiment far more successfully than might have been the case." The *Variety* reviewer felt otherwise: "At few times was he convincing. The spectacle of Lewis singing 'Kol Nidre' in blackface just about 24 hours after the Day of Atonement just didn't sit right along acclisiastical [*sic*] lines, and looked like a dramatic gimmick of a bygone era."[8] In July 1974, plans were announced for an all-new, all-black musical production of *The Jazz Singer*, under the management of New York record producer Barbara Gittler, with lyrics and music by Stephen H. Lemberg and book by Charles L. Russell, to appear on Broadway the following spring. In this version, the setting was to have been 125th Street instead of the Lower East Side, but the action would take place in the late 1920s and the conflict would involve a gospel preacher and his ragtime-singing son.

Despite the success of similar efforts like *The Wiz*, nothing further has been heard of this production. At the time of this writing, however, announcement was made that rock singer Neil Diamond had just signed a record four-million-dollar contract with Paramount to star in and write songs for yet another film remake of *The Jazz Singer*. Whether this latest version materializes, it is not likely that we have seen the last of the jazz singer story— not so long as there are socially, economically, and culturally distinct segments of American society with strong aspirations for the future and equally strong ties to their pasts.[9]

8. *Variety*, October 21, 1959, p. 48.

9. The information in this essay was derived principally from materials in the Samson Raphaelson Collection, University Archives, University of Illinois at Urbana-Champaign; Theatre Collection, Library of the Performing Arts at Lincoln Center, New York Public Library; the Warner Brothers Collection, Cinema Library, University of Southern California; the Warner Film Library, Wisconsin Center for Film and Theater Research, University of Wisconsin–Madison; and from contemporary trade publications, especially *Variety*, *Moving Picture World*, and *Motion Picture News*.

1. *"The New York ghetto—throbbing to that rhythm of music which is older than civilization."*

2. *"Sara Rabinowitz. God made her a Woman and Love made her a Mother."*

3. *"See them shuffle along—"*

4. *"My son was to stand at my side and sing tonight—but now I have no son."*

5. "Jakie Rabinowitz had become Jack Robin—*the cantor's son, a* jazz singer. *But fame was still an uncaptured bubble.*"

6. "Maybe he's fallen in love with a shiksa."

7. *"He hasn't a chance with Mary."*

8. *"Never saw the sun shinin' so bright—"*

9. *"You dare to bring your jazz songs into my house?"*

10. *"Now let's put some life into it—and don't be afraid of bustin' anything."*

11. "He's one of those I-knew-you-when guys—says his name is Noodleson."

12. "I taught you to sing the songs of Israel—to take my place in the synagogue."

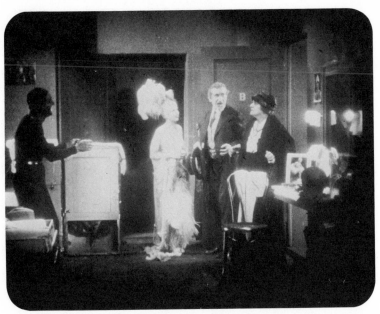

13. *"Jakie—this ain't you?"*

14. *"Maybe your Papa is dying—maybe he won't ever hear you sing again."*

15. *"My son—I love you—"*

16. *"Were you lying when you said your career came before* everything?*"*

17. *"—a jazz singer—singing to his God."*

18. *"Mammy!"*

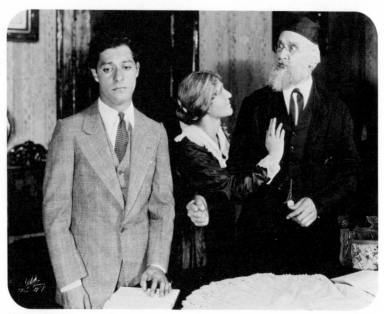

19. *George Jessel, Dorothy Raymond, and Howard Lang in the* Jazz Singer *play. (Theatre Collection, Library of the Performing Arts at Lincoln Center)*

20. *Jessel in blackface with Dorothy Raymond and Sam Jaffe as Yudelson in the* Jazz Singer *play. (Theatre Collection, Library of the Performing Arts at Lincoln Center)*

21. *Jessel as Jack Robin with two girls from the show in the* Jazz Singer *play. (Theatre Collection, Library of the Performing Arts at Lincoln Center)*

22. *The rehearsal scene in act 2 of the* Jazz Singer *play. (Theatre Collection, Library of the Performing Arts at Lincoln Center)*

23. *Jessel with Dorothy Raymond, Tony Kennedy as the doctor, and Sam Jaffe in the* Jazz Singer *play. (Theatre Collection, Library of the Performing Arts at Lincoln Center)*

24. *Mildred Dunnock, Danny Thomas, and Eduard Franz in a production still from the 1952* Jazz Singer. *(Museum of Modern Art/Film Stills Archive)*

25. *Danny Thomas and Peggy Lee in a production still from the 1952* Jazz Singer. *(Museum of Modern Art/Film Stills Archive)*

26. On the set for Vitaphone shooting at Warner Brothers. Soundproof camera booths in background. (Courtesy of John Mullin)

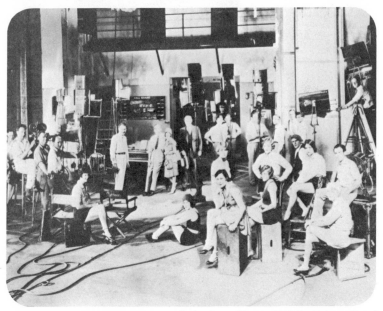

27. Director and cast on the set of The Jazz Singer (1927). (International Museum of Photography)

SIMPLEX PROJECTOR

4 - TURNTABLE EQUIPMENT
(4-A) PEDESTAL BASE
(4-B) COUPLING
(4-C) RECORD CLAMP
(4-D) GUARD
5 - REPRODUCER

3 - PROJECTOR DRIVING MECHANISM
(3-A) GEAR BOX
(3-B) EXTENSIBLE SHAFT
(3-C) BEVEL GEAR BOX FOR SIMPLEX PROJECTOR
2 - CONTROL BOX

1 - MOTOR
(1-A) MOTOR BASE

28. *Vitaphone theater sound apparatus attached to Simplex projector. (Courtesy of Anthony Slide) See pages 184–88 for description.*

The Jazz Singer

Adaptation and Continuity
by
ALFRED A. COHN

From the stage play by
SAMSON RAPHAELSON

The Jazz Singer

TITLE 1:   The New York ghetto, the daily life of which throbs
to the rhythm of music that is as old as civilization.

FADE IN

1.   EXT. NEW YORK STREET   LONG SHOT
It is a typical East Side business street at the height of the
day's activities, a street that is lined with pushcarts,
sidewalk vendors and little stores, with its milling shop-
pers, its petty marketing arguments, its unkempt kids
playing in the street heedless of consequences. In the distance is seen an elevated train flashing across the background like a comet across the sky.

2.   MOVING SHOT   SAME
A shot may be made from an auto or truck down the street
showing the teeming life of the ghetto. As the camera
reaches a street intersection, a half dozen kids come into the
scene.

3.   MED. SHOT   KIDS (STUDIO STREET)
They are playing tag on the intersecting street which is
given over to tenements. There are no pushcarts and only a
few stores in the basements or ground floors of the buildings which house many thousands of ghetto folk. The kids
are attracted to something. They all look down the street
and then start running in the direction they have been
looking. Some little girls join them. (Vitaphone street
piano, at some distance.)[1]

4.   EXT. SIDE STREET   MED. SHOT
In front of a low brick building is an Italian with a street
piano and he is grinding out that always popular classic of

the East Side, "The Sidewalks of New York." The kids come into the scene and gather around the hurdy-gurdy.

5.   CLOSE-UP GROUP
The Italian smiles as the children start dancing about. He looks expectantly at the windows above him and nods pleasantly to someone up above as he continues cranking the piano.

6.   EXT. TENEMENTS LONG SHOT
Looking upward from the street piano. This may be a very effective shot. In several of the windows women are looking down at the music-maker and other heads appear in other windows. Several take deliberate aim and toss coins to the street.

7.   CLOSE-UP ITALIAN
He holds out his ragged cap and expertly catches several coins without once taking his hand from the crank of the street piano. The piece ends. He pulls a little lever and starts turning on another selection—some old operatic favorite like the "Intermezzo" from *Cavalleria Rusticana*. He starts moving down the street as he plays.

8.   TENEMENT STREET LONG SHOT
As the street piano, still in operation, goes down the street, the group of kids, now much larger, follows along. The Italian stops in front of another building, which adjoins the Orchard Street synagogue.

9.   CLOSE SHOT FRONT SYNAGOGUE
It bears the name, in Hebrew, of the temple. Several children get up on the steps in front of the closed doors to listen to the music, which is approaching. Next door is an old brownstone front, before which the Italian stops. Underneath is a store, and in the flat over the store live Cantor Rabinowitz and his family.

10.   INT. ROOM IN SYNAGOGUE
Full shot of the little anteroom in which the rabbi holds
school for the children of the congregation and in which the
cantor teaches the boys of the choir the songs and chants of
the orthodox—the prayers set to music that has been
handed down for generations. Several boys are seated on a
bench beside a battered old square piano (one of the old
square Knabes may be obtained here). The sound of the
street piano comes through the open window, and the kids
rush to the window. They no sooner get to it and climb up
to look out when the door into the room from the
synagogue proper slowly opens and the head of the ven-
erable Cantor Rabinowitz appears.

TITLE 2:   Cantor Rabinowitz, who sang and taught the
youth of his congregation to sing the age-old songs
of Judea—a man revered and respected by all the
ghetto.

11.   CLOSE-UP   CANTOR
He peers into the room to see if his class is ready for him. He
has some difficulty in finding them. Finally he discovers
them at the window. He lifts his head as he hears the strains
from the street piano, and a look of disgust comes to him.
He closes the door behind him and starts in with a determined look.

11A.   REVERSE SHOT   BOYS
They are packed in the window, patched pants seats and
legs only being visible.

12.   EXT.   MED. SHOT
The Italian is now in front of the synagogue and is grinding
out another tune while the children dance about the dis-
cordant instrument.

13.   INT. SCHOOL ROOM   MED. SHOT
The four or five boys are jammed into the open window,

some of them half way out with feet sticking almost straight out backward. With determined tread the cantor comes up behind them and starts yanking them out of the window. They are badly frightened and duck as the cantor cuffs them right and left.

14.   FULL SHOT   ROOM

The boys, some of them propelled from behind by the irate cantor, scramble for their seats. The cantor starts to come after them, then the strains of the music assault his delicate ear and he turns instead to the window.

15.   CLOSE-UP   CANTOR

He takes hold of the window and yanks it down roughly as though he cannot shut out the sound from without quickly enough. (Vitaphone music quickly dimmed to just a faint sound.) Then he turns and faces the boys. He looks them over, muttering to himself imprecations on the terrible sounds from without—an insult to his musically attuned ear.

16.   MED. SHOT   BOYS AND CANTOR

The boys straighten up with solemn looks on their faces as the cantor looks them over scowlingly.

17.   EXT. STREET OUTSIDE TEMPLE   LONG SHOT

The Italian and his piano are disappearing in the distance, and a group of boys are playing ball in the street. One is batting.

18.   INT. CANTOR   CLOSE-UP

He is looking at the boys as he says:

TITLE 3:   "Where is Jakie, my son?"

19.   FULL SHOT   ROOM

The cantor is in the foreground addressing the boys. As he finishes the question one of the boys starts to answer it. The old man suddenly jumps around and looks up in back of him.

20. CLOSE-UP   WINDOW
There is a big round hole in the window.

21. CLOSE-UP   CANTOR
He looks down at the glass on the floor, then stoops and picks up a ball from the floor. He shakes his head ominously. He scowls at the kids, then looks toward the door.

22. CLOSE-UP   AT DOOR
It is opening cautiously and the black curly head of a boy of about thirteen appears. He enters hesitatingly and fearfully of the possible consequences.

23. FULL SHOT   ROOM
The kids all look from father to son expectantly, each hoping that Jakie will get a licking as soon as possible. The cantor comes toward the boy, his brows knitted in a deep frown. Jakie starts toward his father repeating, "I couldn't help it—I didn't mean to hit it so hard—honest I didn't." They meet in the center of the room, the boy still protesting half tearfully. The old man brings back his arm as though to strike him.

24. CLOSE SHOT   BOTH
As the cantor brings back his arm, Jakie shuts his eyes and ducks, but the cantor reconsiders and brings the hand down alongside without striking the boy. He waves him to his seat on the bench with a half-uttered threat to "fix him good the next time."

25. FULL SHOT   ROOM
The cantor turns from Jakie with an impatient gesture and lines the boys up for their lesson. He calls them to attention, then tells them to listen to what he is going to sing. He walks to the piano and poises a hand over the keys.

26.   CLOSE-UP   CANTOR
He strikes a note to give him the key he wants but the piano
is evidently out of tune. He shakes his head disgustedly,
then takes an old-fashioned tuning fork out of his inside
coat pocket and strikes it on the side of the piano, then
holds it to his ear. He sings the note and then indicates to
the boys that they are to follow him as he sings.

27.   MED. SHOT   CANTOR AND BOYS
The cantor is singing and one of the boys is paying no
attention. He is looking around toward the window long-
ingly. The cantor, still singing, walks over to him and cuffs
him on the ear.

28.   CLOSE-UP   CANTOR AND BOY
The boy ducks a second swipe. The cantor glares at him and
demands that he give his undivided attention to the lesson.

29.   CLOSE SHOT   OTHER BOYS
They are singing but taking in the scene on the side. They
grin at each other in joy at their companion's trouble, then
they quickly turn their eyes forward and sing more lustily
as they feel the cantor's eyes on them.

30.   FULL SHOT   ROOM
The cantor takes his place again. He shows his disgust with
the manner in which the boys are singing and, with an
impatient gesture, he stops and tells them to go home.

31.   CLOSE-UP   CANTOR
He waves them away, saying:

TITLE 4:   "Go now, you sound like crazy cats crying already."

32.   MED. SHOT   GROUP
The cantor finishes his dismissal and as the boys, including
Jakie, start for the door, he stops his son. Jakie, with a

crestfallen look, follows with his eyes the disappearing figures of his playmates, who quickly exit. His father calls him and he comes opposite him and looks up rather sullenly for the scolding he expects.

33. CLOSE-UP   CANTOR AND SON
The cantor looks down at Jakie with a scowl and starts berating him. He points to the window and his anger again rises. Jakie starts backing away as though expecting violence. The old man gets himself together and his attitude changes from anger to sadness. He says to the boy:

TITLE 5:   "A fine cantor you are going to be—smeshing synagogue windows yet!"

The boy looks up at him with an effort, which reflects something of the length of time he has thought about this unpleasant future. He blurts out:

TITLE 6:   "But Papa, I don't want to be no cantor."

The father looks at him as though not willing to believe his ears. He has never heard anything quite so blasphemous. He gulps a few times and then, with a grimly sarcastic smile, he says:

TITLE 7:   "And if not a cantor, what are you going to be?"

He looks at the boy, awaiting an answer to a question which he regards as unanswerable.

34. CLOSE-UP   BOY
He swallows a few times, then looking up at his father courageously, he declares:

TITLE 8:   "I want to be a singer in a theayter."

He half ducks as if expecting a blow.

35. CLOSE-UP   CANTOR
He looks at the boy in amazement, his hands going aloft in horror. It is difficult for him to speak. Finally he breaks out:

TITLE 9:   "For five generations there has been a Rabinowitz
            as cantor—I have taught you to be one—"

He pauses for a breath, then, sticking out his bristling
beard in the boy's direction, he almost yells:

TITLE 10:   "And *you*—you want to be a common actor in a
            lowlife theayter! "

36. CLOSE-UP   FATHER AND SON
The father makes as though to strike the boy, who this time
stands his ground bravely. The hand of the aged man is
raised for the blow, but he halts it in mid air. The father
looks down into the eyes of the boy, which are fixed stead-
fastly on him. He shakes his head sorrowfully.

                                                FADE OUT

FADE IN

37. INT. MULLER'S CAFE
Long shot discloses one of those places so common in New
York before Prohibition, a long bar in front, and behind,
separated from the bar by a partition and swinging doors, a
"garden" approachable from the "family entrance" where
"ladies" may dine and drink their beer, whether with es-
corts or without them. The back of the place can be seen
faintly. The bar is being well patronized, and the three
German bartenders are busy putting out huge schooners of
the amber fluid. Waiters are going in and out of the swinging doors.

38. INT. GARDEN   FULL SHOT
Looking toward the bar, there is a battered old piano in the
foreground on a slightly raised platform, at which sits a
young man who looks twice his age because of dissipation.
He is smoking a cigarette in a listless manner, and there is a
schooner of beer on the piano at the end of the keyboard.
He is running his hands over the keys as though playing to
himself. Back of him may be seen the diners and drinkers.
There is an occasional family group and several of the tables

are occupied by flashily dressed women of an obviously well-known occupation. Some are accompanied by men. At other tables are men alone quietly drinking.

39. CLOSE-UP   FAMILY ENTRANCE
Seen from the inside, the door opens slowly and the head of Jakie Rabinowitz appears. He looks about as though to see if the coast is clear, then enters. His attitude indicates that he has been there before.

40. FULL SHOT   GARDEN
Jakie threads his way among the tables to the piano. Several of the drinkers look at him as they recognize the boy, and there is some conversation about him among the groups. Jakie calls to the piano player, who swings around to greet him, as he gets on the platform.

41. CLOSE SHOT   PLAYER AND JAKIE
The pianist greets Jakie jocularly:

TITLE 11:   "Well how's the kid Caruso today?"

Jakie answers him in kind:

TITLE 12:   "Great! How's old kid Paderooski?"

They laugh and the piano player indicates the diners and drinkers, saying that maybe there's a few dimes for the kid in the place. They confer a moment, then the piano player whirls around and strikes a chord.

42. FULL SHOT   GARDEN
Those at the tables look toward the piano with interest as Jakie, in the background, is seen standing on the little platform facing them.

43. MED. SHOT   BOY AND PIANO PLAYER
The player plays the introduction to "Mighty Lak a Rose" and the boy starts to sing. (The various shots for this will

have to be in accordance with Vitaphone technique and its necessities.) Vitaphone singing stops, when cut is made.

FADE IN

44.   INT. RABINOWITZ LIVING ROOM   DAY

It is a rather large room for that locality, the living room and dining room of the modest flat occupied by the cantor and his family. The furniture is good but old, and there are many shelves and tables which are filled with knick-knacks, china, glassware, and silver. Mrs. Rabinowitz, a sweet-faced, motherly woman of between forty-five and fifty, is just setting the table. It is the day of the eve of Atonement Day, the most important holiday of Judaism, which is observed by even the least religious of Jews, by twenty-four hours of abstinence from food or drink. The cantor is pacing up and down the room in a very nervous manner. He pauses occasionally to make a quick remark, punctuated by an elaborate gesture, then resumes his pacing. The subject of his remarks is Jakie.

TITLE 13:   Sara Rabinowitz was not as learned in the lore of her race as her husband, but she had a deeper and better understanding of life—and Jakie.

45.   CLOSE-UP   MOTHER

She is setting plates on the table as she listens to the cantor. She hesitates, then says:

TITLE 14:   "Jakie is a good boy, Papa—but maybe he shouldn't be a cantor."

46.   MED. SHOT   BOTH

As Sara finishes title and resumes her work, the cantor stops and looks at her in amazement. He starts to say: "*What*, not a cantor, you say that?" Then he takes a long breath and, bringing his fist down through the air, he breaks out into a stream of Yiddish.

47. CLOSE-UP   CANTOR
    He declares violently that Jakie must be a cantor, just like himself and his fathers before him. He leans closer to his wife as he says, with some semblance of pride:

TITLE 15:   "He knows all the songs and prayers even now so good as I do. He could take my place yet tonight and sing 'Kol Nidre' when Yom Kippur begins."

He pauses as though awaiting an answer to what he considers an unanswerable argument.

48. CLOSE-UP   SARA
    She nods her head in acquiescence of what her husband has said; then she shakes her head slowly and replies:

TITLE 16:   "He has it all in his head, yes, but it is not in his heart. He is of America."

49. CLOSE SHOT   BOTH
    As she finishes the old man looks at her in horror. This which she has said is, to him, treason. She turns her back as he begins to scold breathlessly.

50. FULL SHOT   CAFE FROM FRONT END OF BAR
    (Vitaphone singing is resumed.) There are only a few people drinking at the bar in the foreground. The "garden" is visible as people pass through the swinging doors.

51. FULL SHOT   GARDEN
    As seen from the doors, Jakie is singing and the people at the tables are watching and listening approvingly.

52. MED. SHOT   BAR
    A tall, spare Hebrew with a straggly beard and a cutaway coat comes into the foreground. He orders a glass of beer, putting his nickel on the bar as he does so.

53.   CLOSE-UP   YUDELSON
He drinks slowly and with relish.

TITLE 17:   Moisha Yudelson, a man of influence in the business and religious affairs of the ghetto.

Back. He reaches over and takes some of the free lunch. His
attention is attracted to the music. He listens curiously,
then starts for the door to the garden.

54.   MED. SHOT   DOOR
Yudelson pushes the swinging door open, his glass of beer
in one hand and a slice of meat on a piece of bread in the
other. His eyes bulge as he sees the singer.

55.   LONG REVERSE SHOT
Jakie is singing.

56.   CLOSE-UP   YUDELSON
His lips tighten. He determines that something must be
done about this and he knows just what it is. He goes
quickly to the bar.

57.   MED. SHOT   BAR
Yudelson gulps down the beer, crams the rest of the food
into his mouth, and exits. (Vitaphone singing stops.)

58.   INT. RABINOWITZ HOME
The cantor is walking up and down the floor nervously.
Sara is putting the dishes of food on the table. The cantor
stops and faces Sara sternly.

59.   CLOSE-UP   CANTOR
He takes out a huge silver watch, looks at it, and says:

TITLE 18:   "Tonight Jakie is to sing 'Kol Nidre' in school and
he isn't yet here."

He snaps shut the watch and glares at Sara.

60.   MED. SHOT   BOTH
Sara makes some excuse for the boy. Maybe he doesn't know what time it is. He starts pacing up and down again. Sara finishes the placing of food on the table and starts arranging the chairs.

61.   CLOSE-UP   CANTOR
He scowls as he pauses in his pacing and says:

TITLE   19:   "If he don't come now in a minute, he starts his Yom Kippur fasting without supper." [2]

62.   FULL SHOT   ROOM
As the cantor resumes his pacing, Sara hears someone at the door and goes to it, only to admit, instead of the expected Jakie, an excited Yudelson. The cantor turns around in surprise. Yudelson rushes up to him and starts telling him about seeing Jakie singing nigger songs in Muller's. [3] The cantor throws up his hands in horror. Yudelson nods grimly but in a satisfied manner.

63.   CLOSE-UP   YUDELSON
He says in a self-righteous manner:

TITLE   20:   "Of course it ain't any of mine business, but I say to myself it's my duty, I—"

He looks around surprised.

64.   FULL SHOT   ROOM
The cantor has grabbed his hat and is on his way out of the door as Yudelson stands open-mouthed. Sara starts wringing her hands.

65.   CLOSE SHOT   YUDELSON AND SARA
As they see the cantor disappear, Sara looks at Yudelson with marked disapproval. He decides that it is time to go and turns as Sara starts to reprove him for his tattling. She tells him he would be better off attending to his own business. With a hurried excuse Yudelson turns.

66.   FULL SHOT   ROOM

Yudelson quickly disappears out of the front door and Sara
drops into a chair heavily. She knows that there will be an
unpleasant scene before long and she dreads it.

67.   INT. BEER HALL   FULL SHOT

Jakie is just finishing a song and those at the tables start
applauding. Some of them throw coins to Jakie.

68.   CLOSE-UP   JAKIE

His singing manners have gone. Now he is just business as
he starts to pick up the scattered coins. He picks up the last
one and pockets it. Then he turns to the piano player.

69.   CLOSE SHOT   BOTH

They discuss what Jakie is to sing next. Then the piano
player starts a ragtime piece and Jakie starts to sing in the
most approved darkey manner.

70.   FULL SHOT   GARDEN

The people at the tables are showing new interest in the
singer.

71.   CLOSE SHOT   FAMILY ENTRANCE

The door opens suddenly and the figure of the irate cantor
appears. He pauses and takes one look, then strides in with
great determination.

72.   MED. SHOT   JAKIE FROM FRONT

He is putting everything he has into his song. He is rolling
his eyes and calling on "his baby." His eyes drop and he
looks forward just in time to see his father coming toward
him. His voice breaks as the old man comes into the scene.
A determined arm reaches up and grabs him, and the song
ends abruptly.

73.   FULL SHOT   ROOM

With the boy in a viselike grip, the cantor starts toward the door with the squirming figure of his young son. The people at the table are laughing heartily at the unexpected entertainment. Father and son exit.

74. CLOSE-UP PIANO PLAYER
Getting the humor of the situation, he starts playing something appropriate, like "Stay in Your Own Backyard" or perhaps something more modern and more to the point.

75. RABINOWITZ LIVING ROOM
Sara is sitting in the rocking chair, rocking slowly back and forth, occasionally dabbing at her eyes with a handkerchief. She gets up and goes to the table. She feels one of the dishes and, seeing that it is cold, she starts with it to the kitchen. As she returns she looks toward the front door, then rushes hurriedly in that direction.

76. MED. SHOT FRONT DOOR
The cantor comes in breathlessly, pushing the boy ahead of him, just as Sara comes up to them. The boy tries to go to her but the irate cantor holds him tightly and motions Sara not to interfere.

77. CLOSE SHOT GROUP
The cantor glares down at the boy who starts squirming. He tightens his grip on him as he repeats over and over: "Singing nigger songs in a beer garden! You bummer! You no good lowlife!" As Sara tries to intercede, the cantor silences her almost roughly. As he half pushes her away he says:

TITLE 21:   "I will teach him he shall never again use his voice for such low things."

He takes a fresh grip on the boy and starts in the direction of the bedroom.

78. FULL SHOT ROOM
As father with son in tow go toward the bedroom, the

mother follows a few steps, pleading with the cantor not to whip Jakie. He turns around and demands what she means by such interference. She looks at him imploringly.

79.   CLOSE-UP   SARA
She holds out her outstretched hands to the cantor, saying:

TITLE 22:   "It will do no good, Papa—and he must get ready for school in a few minutes. Yom Kippur begins soon."

80.   CLOSE SHOT   GROUP
The cantor answers her with a snort of disgust and renewed determination to continue with what he considers his duty. The boy, emboldened by his mother's championship, turns and faces his father courageously. The old man looks down at him in surprise.

81.   CLOSE-UP   CANTOR AND SON
The boy looks up at his father, his boyish face set with determination. He declares:

TITLE 23:   "I told you before—if you whip me again, I'll run away—and never come back."

At this show of rebellion the cantor stiffens. He nods his head menacingly as though accepting the challenge, takes another grip on the boy's shoulder, and pushes him toward the bedroom, as Jakie starts sobbing hysterically. At the door, the cantor takes a strap that is hanging over a chair near the door.

82.   MED. SHOT   ROOM
As the cantor shoves open the door, Sara again tries to intervene. The cantor holds out a hand to prevent her following, pushes Jakie into the bedroom, and follows him, closing the door behind him with a bang. Sara stands looking tearfully at the door, realizing the expected crisis in the little family, which she has feared, has finally arrived.

83.   CLOSE-UP   SARA
She stands mutely facing the door. Suddenly she starts and
listens, then puts her hands over her ears as though to shut
out the sounds she hears, and her shoulders heave with
repressed sobs. She starts for the door, then restrains herself. Her emotions finally overcome her and she drops into
a chair and cries without restraint. (Nothing of what occurs
in the bedroom is shown.)

84.   MED. SHOT   SAME
The door of the bedroom opens suddenly and Jakie
emerges. He is shaking with a mixture of anger and the
painful effects of the whipping. He comes out quickly,
looks at his mother, rushes over, and kisses her impulsively,
and as she puts her arms around him, he breaks away and
before she can stop him, he runs toward the front door.

85.   FULL SHOT   ROOM
Jakie rushes to the door and dashes out, as the cantor
appears in the doorway of the bedroom. He is somewhat
breathless from exertion. He does not look to see what has
become of the boy. He pauses and looks at his wife in a
dazed way. He looks toward the door. Then in a mechanical
way he takes his watch from his pocket and glances at it.

86.   CLOSE-UP   CANTOR
He holds the watch up to his eyes closely, then looks in the
direction of his wife and says:

TITLE   24:   "It is time for the services, Mama."

      . He turns to the wall behind him where hangs the prayer
shawl and the freshly washed and ironed robe which the
cantor wears when he sings the "Kol Nidre" on the Day of
Atonement.

87.   MED. SHOT   BOTH
The cantor starts putting on the robe, with great delibera-

tion. Sara is standing mutely looking toward the door through which her boy vanished.

FADE OUT

FADE IN

88. INT. SYNAGOGUE   LONG SHOT
Every pew in the place is filled with men, and in the balcony behind sit the women in the place reserved for them. On the raised platform, the cantor and the choir boys are taking their places.

89. CLOSE SHOT   CANTOR AND CHOIR
As the boys line up, a solemn look on each young face, the cantor looks from one to the other.

90. CLOSE-UP   CANTOR
He has his back to the congregation. He has his eyes fixed on the place where Jakie usually has stood.

91. MED. SHOT
As the cantor stands motionless, the rabbi steps up to him. The old man looks at him and they exchange a few words.

92. CLOSE SHOT   BOTH
The cantor looks at the vacant place again, then turns to the rabbi and says, with a break in his voice:

TITLE 25:   "Tonight my boy Jakie was to sing 'Kol Nidre'—but he is not going to be a cantor now."

Back. He finishes title. The rabbi moves out of scene, and the cantor takes the position in which he is to sing.

93. FULL SHOT   SYNAGOGUE
The congregation comes to attention, and small groups that have been conversing look toward the cantor.

94. MED. SHOT   CHOIR
The cantor is in the foreground, his back to the camera, as

the first low notes of the "Kol Nidre" are sung. Never has the cantor's voice sung the heart-breaking song like this before. There is a tear in every note, and as his voice rises in the wailing harmony that is handed down from the walls of Jerusalem, the choir boys look at him in wonder. (Vitaphone is used in full volume.)[4]

95. FULL SHOT   SYNAGOGUE
As the cantor's voice rises in a long, mournful wail, the scene and music slowly FADE.

TITLE 26:   Ten years and three thousand miles away from the ghetto.

FADE IN

96. AIRPLANE VIEW OF SAN FRANCISCO
A shot may be obtained which immediately identifies the city, with its hills and ferries and the Golden Gate in the distance.

DISSOLVE INTO:

97. OFFICE STAR VAUDEVILLE CIRCUIT
Full shot of room shows various types of performers seated about the room awaiting an opportunity to talk to the booking manager. There is an old-time legitimate actor of the East Lynne period, a dancing team of girls, three Teutonic-looking acrobats, a fat young man whose clothes were once quite "snappy," and a few other types found usually in such a place. The fat man is hidden behind a copy of *Variety*. An office boy, small, weazened, and wise beyond his years, pertly tells all inquirers that Mr. Schuler is "in conference." All of the people in the room look hopefully toward the door every time it is opened and look away hopelessly every time it closes. A big, husky, flashily dressed blonde enters and breezes up to the boy. He gets up and tries to hold the gate of the enclosure shut, so that she cannot enter.

98.   CLOSE-UP   BLONDE AND BOY
She says that she is there to see Mr. Schuler. The boy looks
at her and says:

TITLE 27:   "Mr. Schuler's in conf'rence and can't be disturbed."

The girl gives him a supercilious look, shoves him aside,
and sweeps up to the door to the inner room. She opens it
and passes in as the boy stands with open mouth and gazes
after her.

99.   FULL SHOT   ROOM
The less fortunate performers sit and look wonderingly at
the closed door. The boy finally shrugs his shoulders and
takes his chair. The outer door opens and a young man
enters. He is shabbily dressed and, although he is neat of
person, it is obvious that he is down on his luck. He pauses
and then hesitatingly goes up to the railing where the office
boy sits idly hammering a typewriter with no paper in it.
The boy doesn't even look up.

100.   CLOSE-UP   JACK
He stands looking at the boy nervously.

TITLE 28:   It was a long jump from Jakie Rabinowitz to Jack
Robin—and the roses in his pathway were almost
hidden under the thorns.
                                        —George Jessel[5]

Back to scene. Jack asks the boy if he can see Mr. Schuler.

101.   CLOSE SHOT   BOTH
The boy just looks up and snaps out that "it can't be
done—he's in an important conf'rence." Jack hopelessly
turns away and the boy continues his mauling of the
typewriter.

102.   FULL SHOT   ROOM
As Jack walks disconsolately over to the one vacant chair,

the young man hidden behind the copy of *Variety* looks up. He recognizes Jack and, with a smile, he jumps up and they grab each other's hands.

103.   CLOSE-UP   BOTH
They exchange the usual greeting: "If it ain't my old partner of the sticks, Jack Robin!" and Jack's return:

TITLE 29:   "—and the last time I saw you Buster Billings, you were getting ready to climb a side door Pullman in Cheyenne."

Back to scene. They reminisce some more. Jack asks him what he is doing, and Buster points hopelessly to the door of the inner office, saying, "The same thing you are."

104.   FULL SHOT   ROOM
As they are talking, the boy suddenly jumps up as though answering a buzzer and goes to the inner door. He opens it, listens to something said within, nods, and closes the door. He walks to the rail and gives the people sitting around the room a contemptuous look.

105.   CLOSE-UP   BOY
He pauses a moment as he feels the expectant eyes on him, and with the cruelty of youth, he barks out at them:

TITLE 30:   "The boss ain't seeing anybody else today—you can all duck."

106.   FULL SHOT   ROOM
The occupants start getting up wearily. They start for the door. Jack and Buster are the last to go. They pause in the doorway.

107.   CLOSE SHOT   BOTH
They look at each other and Jack says to him: "Where to?" Buster pauses and says they can take a walk and stall around awhile. He adds:

TITLE 31:   "Later we'll go to Coffee Dan's. My old side kick,
              Frank James, is the—impresario down there and
              we can bum a feed off him."

They start out of the door.

FADE OUT

108. EXT. STREET
      In the near foreground looking down the street is the en-
      trance to the Orpheum theater. The electric sign in front is
      lighted. The lighted sign is suddenly extinguished to indi-
      cate that the show is over, and people start coming out of
      the doors. This DISSOLVES INTO:

109. INT. THEATER BACKSTAGE   FULL SHOT
      The players who have just finished their act, the closing one
      on the bill, a troupe of acrobats, are just going to their
      dressing rooms. A door to one of the stage dressing rooms
      opens, and a girl dressed neatly in street attire comes half-
      way out.

110. CLOSE-UP   GIRL
      She is a small blonde girl, dressed in excellent taste. She is
      calling out to someone not in sight.

TITLE 32:   Mary Dale, of the "Little Follies" act, was not yet a
              headliner in her own right, but ambition pointed
              the way to fame.

111. MED. SHOT   GIRL
      She comes out of the door and closes it behind her. She calls
      again, and in the background another girl and a young
      man, Ben Thorpe, appear. The girl is a tall, wise-looking
      blonde of about twenty-five and the young man is tall,
      blond, and good-looking. They come up to Mary and there
      is some talk as to where they are going.

112. CLOSE SHOT   THREE
They argue a while, then Mary says: "Let's go over to Coffee Dan's." Estelle says that she won't remain long. The young man takes each by an arm and they start out.[6]

FADE OUT

FADE IN

113. INT. COFFEE DAN'S   FULL SHOT
The tables are pretty well filled by a fairly well-dressed crowd. Some even are in evening clothes. There is a general air of hilarity, but no drinking is in evidence. Next to a table filled by people in evening clothes, their women bedecked with diamonds, is a table at which sit several tough-looking characters. But there are not many of these. Men waiters dash back and forth carrying mostly ham and eggs, the pièce de résistance of a Coffee Dan meal. At the piano on the platform sits Frank James, tortoise shell-bespectacled musician and entertainer as well as master of ceremonies. In the background, up near the platform, is a small table at which sit Jack Robin and Buster Billings.

114. CLOSE-UP   TABLE
Jack and Buster are eating heartily with all the gusto that characterizes a healthy appetite that has been whetted by lengthy fasting. They look up at Frank and grin happily.

115. CLOSE-UP   FRANK
He looks down at them, gives them a signal, then walks to the edge of the platform nearest them.

116. FULL SHOT   ROOM
Frank is trying to get the diners to be quiet. The people at the tables gradually hush their noise. Jack and Buster shove their plates away in complete satisfaction.

117. CLOSE-UP   FRANK
He has a hand upraised as he looks over the crowd. Then he casts a look down at Jack's table and winks as he starts announcing:

TITLE 33:   "And now I am going to ask Mr. Jack Robin to sing
something. Mr. Robin is the famous tenor from
Petaluma."

Back to scene. He winks again as he looks down at the table.

118.   CLOSE SHOT   TABLE
Jack is shrinking back in an embarrassed manner. Buster
reaches over and claps him on the back, telling him to be a
good sport, that they all do it there, even the big ones in
grand opera.

119.   MED. SHOT   TABLES
The people at the tables are looking at Jack and hammering
on the tables with their hammers in an encouraging manner.

120.   CLOSE-UP   JACK AND BUSTER
Jack dumbly accuses Buster of framing him, but the latter
just laughs. Jack finally pulls himself together as he realizes
that there is no out for him.

121.   MED. SHOT   TABLE AND PLATFORM
As Frank leans down with hand extended, Jack stands up,
straightens his coat, and joins him. Frank gives him a hand
and yanks him up on the platform, where they go into a
conference as to what Jack is to sing.

122.   LONG SHOT   FROM PLATFORM
Jack and Frank are in the foreground at the piano talking. In
the background, a group appears at the foot of the stairs just
entering the place. It is the group from the vaudeville
theater. Mary is in front, and as the head waiter motions to
them, they enter the place and are seated at a table just in
front of the platform as Frank sits down at the piano and
starts playing for Jack, who has advanced to the edge of the
platform.

123.   CLOSE-UP   JACK

He starts to sing his song. (The song, which is to be Vita-phoned, should be one especially written for the occasion, as any current number would be out of date long before the picture has played every theater equipped for Vitaphone by release time.)

124.   MED. SHOT   FROM FLOOR

The table at which Mary and her party are seated is in the immediate foreground. They are paying attention only to the waiter who is standing over them awaiting their orders, as Jack is singing. Mary, attracted by his voice, looks away from the group wonderingly as she listens.

125.   CLOSE-UP   MARY

She is looking up at Jack curiously as she listens. This is something new to her.

126.   CLOSE-UP   JACK

He is singing, his eyes aimed toward the back of the place. As though feeling the attraction of Mary's gaze, his eyes slowly come down. As they meet those of Mary, he gulps and almost breaks. With an effort, he continues singing, his eyes on the girl.

127.   CLOSE SHOT   GROUP AT TABLE

Mary still has her eyes on the singer. The others of the group, Estelle and Ben Thorpe, are looking at Jack as they see him looking intently at Mary. They turn to her and start kidding her about her conquest. She kids them in return and does not look at Jack again. She is again her usually reserved self, a girl intensely interested in her work and wrapped up in her career.

128.   MED. SHOT   JACK

He is bringing his song to a close. As he does, Frank gets up quickly and shakes hands with him. Jack is embarrassed at this and, at Frank's instigation, he turns and bows to the audience and jumps down from the platform hurriedly as though in fear that he would be called on again.

129.   FULL SHOT   ROOM
The diners are applauding and pounding on the tables with their hammers. Jack, in the background, is seen going to his table, where Buster rises and slaps him on the back and compliments him on his work. The diners are still applauding and Jack turns and bows to them. Buster tries to get him to go up again but he shakes his head and sits down at his table.

130.   CLOSE-UP   JACK AND BUSTER
Buster is still complimenting Jack, but the latter's eyes have wandered to the table occupied by Mary and her companions. Buster follows his gaze. His face lights up with recognition. Jack notes this and turning to him eagerly says: "Do you know her?" Buster says: "Which her?" Jack indicates Mary. Buster nods: "Sure I know her—I'm going over and say Hello." Jack starts to follow, then subsides, his eyes on Buster.

131.   CLOSE SHOT   MARY'S TABLE
Mary is saying to Thorpe:

TITLE 34:   "Well, I'm going to tell Berg about him—with a voice like that—"

Buster comes up as she is talking. He shakes hands with Mary and Estelle, and Thorpe is introduced. As they shake hands, Estelle spots Jack and tells Buster to ask Jack over. Buster waves his hand and sits down.

132.   CLOSE-UP   JACK
He sees the signal and jumps up eagerly. Then with an effort to slow down in order to hide his eagerness to meet Mary, he walks slowly over to the table.

74

133.   CLOSE SHOT   MARY'S TABLE
Buster is telling them about Jack, when the latter appears.
Buster presents him, and Mary asks him to sit down in the
chair next to her. He does so. Mary turns to him and asks
him something about himself, first congratulating him on
his singing.

134.   FULL SHOT   ROOM
Frank goes to the piano and starts a dance number. The
couples flock out to the little dancing space. Thorpe asks
Estelle to dance and she gets up. Mary and Jack are deep in
conversation.

135.   CLOSE SHOT   MARY'S TABLE
As Estelle and her escort move away in the dance, Buster
looks at Jack and starts to say something. Neither pays any
attention to him. He makes a facetious excuse, then gets up.
They never notice him leave.

136.   FULL SHOT   ROOM
Buster threads his way through the dancers and climbs up
on the platform. He goes over to Frank and sits down on the
stool alongside of him. Frank starts to talk to him while he is
playing.[7]

137.   CLOSE-UP   JACK AND MARY
Jack thanks her for her approval of his song. Then, after a
moment of embarrassment, Jack tells her that he has seen
her act on the Orpheum. He says:

TITLE 35:   "I caught your act in the Orpheum at Salt Lake—I
think you're great!"

He leans over toward her in a gesture of boyish enthusiasm
rather than one of forwardness. Mary smilingly acknowl-
edges the compliment. She asks him where he played in
that city. Jack replies:

75

TITLE 36:   "Oh, I sang in a movie house there—and I've been
              two weeks getting here."

He pauses and looks at her in a sidelong glance to see if,
knowing the truth about him, she would regard him any
differently. She gives him a quick look of sympathy, then
says:

TITLE 37:   "If you come over to the Orpheum tomorrow at
              2:00, I'd like to introduce you to the manager."

Jack looks at her wonderingly. He has been buffeted about
so much that he has long since lost confidence in his own
ability. He asks Mary eagerly if she thinks he can make the
grade there. The girl nods and says:

TITLE 38:   "I think your voice would get you a long ways on
              the big time—you sing jazz, but it's different—
              there's a tear in it."

Jack looks at her gratefully. He is close to a tear now himself.
The girl smiles at him in a purely impersonal manner as he
reaches out his hand toward hers in an impulsive gesture.
Then he slowly withdraws it without touching hers.

                                                    FADE OUT

FADE IN

138. INT. RABINOWITZ HOME
      The cantor, much older and more feeble than when we last
      saw him, is seated at the table in the living room. His beard
      is almost white and the hair about his temples is white and
      thin. There are deep lines in his face, but a look of resigna-
      tion has taken the place of the indomitable sternness that
      marked his appearance ten years before. At his side is
      standing a little Jewish boy, Moey—a youngster of about
      ten—a typical ghetto child of the underfed, frail build. He
      is singing and the old man is nodding his head in time as he
      does so.

139. CLOSE SHOT   BOTH
The cantor suddenly stops the boy. He tells him that he is singing it wrong. He adds:

TITLE 39:   "You must sing it with a sigh—like you are crying out to your God."

He motions to him to sing it again. The boy tries it and is again stopped, this time more impatiently by the cantor.

140. CLOSE-UP   CANTOR
He looks at the boy and his mind seems to wander. There is a misty look in his eyes as he says:

TITLE 40:   "I wish I had my Jakie here—he could show you how to sing it—he had a voice like a angel."

141. CLOSE SHOT   BOTH
Moey looks up at him curiously. The old man has turned his eyes back into the past and is oblivious to the boy's presence until Moey looks up and says:

TITLE 41:   "He ran away from home, didn't he, your boy?"

The old man looks at the boy, suddenly awakened from his reverie. His face sets and his lips compress as he says, very slowly:

TITLE 42:   "I haven't got any boy."

Back to scene. Moey looks up at him wonderingly. The old man looks away and Moey, boylike, is persistent. He tries it again:

TITLE 43:   "But Mike Lefkowitz says your boy is a singer in a theayter way out west—in Pittsburgh or Buffalo."

The cantor looks down at Moey as though he just faintly hears him. He shakes his head, saying to himself, "I have no boy." Then he rises quickly from the chair and says to the boy:

TITLE 44:   "That is all for today—come back tomorrow."

142.   MED. SHOT   ROOM
The boy starts out of the room at this, and the cantor sits down again and is deep in thought as Moey exits.

FADE OUT

FADE IN
143.   RABINOWITZ LIVING ROOM
Mrs. Rabinowitz is seated in the rocking chair, just opposite and a short distance from Yudelson. Both have aged considerably. Yudelson is better dressed and has more of the air of a prosperous citizen. His beard is neatly trimmed and he wears well-tailored clothes. Mrs. Rabinowitz's hair is grayer and there are deeper lines in her face. She is leaning over, listening to Yudelson who has a letter in his hand from which he is reading.

144.   CLOSE SHOT   BOTH
Yudelson looks up from the letter as he says: "Y' understand what he means?" He starts to explain. But Mrs. Rabinowitz stops him and says:

TITLE 45:   "What else does Jakie say in the letter?"

Yudelson starts to read again. Sara leans over closer so that she won't miss a word.

145.   CLOSE-UP   YUDELSON
He is reading the letter with elaborate gesticulations.

INSERT LETTER

Omaha, June 4th.
Dear Mama:
I thought you would like to know I am getting along great in vaudeville, and maybe I will soon be a headliner, and a wonderful girl whose name is Mary Dale got me my big chance out in 'Frisco. Maybe I will be in New York soon.

Your loving son,
Jakie

P.S. You can write me care State-Lake theater, Chicago. Remember the name is *Jack Robin.*

Back to scene. Yudelson looks up as he finishes reading.

146.   CLOSE SHOT   BOTH
Mrs. Rabinowitz asks Yudelson what Jakie means by head-liner. Yudelson explains, and the old lady is thoughtful a moment.

147.   CLOSE-UP   MOTHER
She hesitates a moment, then turns to Yudelson and says:

TITLE 46:   "Read it again, what he says about the girl."

148.   CLOSE SHOT   BOTH
Yudelson again reads the passage about Mary Dale. He looks at Mrs. Rabinowitz as though realizing what she is thinking of. He says: "Nu, anything else?" Mrs. Rabinowitz hesitates, then says:

TITLE 47:   "Maybe he is fallen in love—and by her name she is a *shiksa*."

Yudelson thinks a moment, then shrugs his shoulders. He says:

TITLE 48:   "Maybe not—you know Jennie Levi on the theay-ter is Genevieve Leeds."

The old lady is relieved at this solution of her problem. Yudelson hands her back the letter. She thanks him and he starts to get up.[8]

FADE OUT

FADE IN
149.   LONG SHOT   BACKSTAGE
It is the stage of the State-Lake theater in Chicago, and a matinee performance is in progress. There is the usual activity among the stagehands preparatory to changing the set. The act which is now on is a dancing act, and there is only a fleeting glimpse of the dancers through the aperture of a narrow entrance. (A novel effect may be had by shooting through the first entrance so that [there is] a view of part

of the audience as well as some of the dancers who are downstage. The dance music may be reproduced by the Vitaphone.)

150.   MED. SHOT   STAGE

Through entrance from another angle there is a more complete view of the dancers. Mary Dale, the principal of the act, is seen doing a movement of her dance. (This should be of such grace and technique that would warrant headline position for Mary.) As the dance comes to a close, a figure comes into the foreground, and a side view shows that it is Jack Robin in blackface. He applauds from the wings as Mary finishes. Apparently he is just ready to go on with his act, or has just finished and is watching Mary before he takes the make-up off his face.

151.   CLOSE-UP   JACK

He is applauding vigorously.

TITLE 49:   Orchard Street would have had some difficulty in recognizing Jakie Rabinowitz of Beth-El choir under the burnt cork of Jack Robin.

Back. He takes a step forward as though to meet the receding dancer as she bows repeatedly in making her exit.

152.   MED. SHOT   SAME

Mary almost backs into Jack as she comes off the stage, and he puts out a hand to catch her arm. The supporting dancers have exited on the other side. There is just time for an exclamation of surprise from Mary as she goes on the stage again for another bow. She turns to Jack as she gets to him and puts a hand on his arm, as he compliments her on her dancing.

153.   CLOSE-UP   JACK AND MARY

She says to Jack with a humorous gleam in her eye:

TITLE 50:   "I don't know what I'd do, Jack, if it wasn't for the encouragement you give me."

She laughs as she says this and Jack, realizing that she is kidding him, says, in a rather embarrassed manner:

TITLE 51:   "Well, you know I'm just crazy about—your act."

It is evident that he loses his nerve as he is about to tell her that it is she he is crazy about. Mary starts for her dressing room, but is suddenly awakened to the fact that the audience is still applauding and she turns quickly to the entrance.

154.   MED. SHOT   SAME
Mary is out on the stage bowing to the audience again. She bows several times as she backs into the narrow space again where Jack awaits her.

155.   FULL SHOT   STAGE
As Jack and Mary walk toward the dressing rooms, several persons on the stage observe them. Two of the girls in the dancing act who are standing at a door on the balcony overlooking the stage look at them and turn to each other.

156.   CLOSE-UP   GIRLS
One of them, indicating Jack and Mary, says to the other:

TITLE 52:   "He's surely goofy about her."

The other one nods and says:

TITLE 53:   "But he ain't got a chance—no Mammy singer for Mary."

Back to scene. One opens the door and they go into girls' dressing room, through the door of which may be seen the girls in various stages of dishabille.

157.   MED. SHOT   JACK AND MARY
They are standing in front of the door of the stage dressing

room. Jack starts to leave, but Mary halts him telling him that she has something to show him. He looks at her wonderingly. She opens the door and darts into the room, returning immediately with a telegram which she hands him.

158.   CLOSE-UP   JACK AND MARY
Jack takes the telegram and looks at it. It reads:

INSERT TELEGRAM

>   NEW YORK
>   Miss Mary Dale
>   State-Lake Theater, Chicago, Ill.
>   Would you consider leading role new musical show Fall opening, rehearsals begin two weeks. Wire answer.
>
>   Harry Lee

Back to scene. Jack's face brightens as he finishes reading it. He hands back the wire to Mary, saying:

TITLE 54:   "Gee, it's a great chance for you."

Mary nods, smilingly telling Jack it's the opportunity she has been working for, ever since she began her professional career. Jack pauses a moment as realization begins to come to him that Mary's good fortune means the end of the happiest period of his life. He puts out a hand and congratulates her, then he adds falteringly:

TITLE 55:   "I'll be sorry . . . in one way to see you go. I . . . we . . . we'll miss you a lot."

Mary smiles tenderly. She puts a hand on his arm affectionately. Jack looks away as he says:

TITLE 56:   "I'll never forget that it is to you I owe everything I am—or ever will be."

Mary affects a light manner as she laughs and tells him to snap out of the gloom. Jack pulls himself out of his sentimental mood to meet her assumed gaiety. He asks her when she is leaving and she says after the night performance the next day.

159. FULL SHOT   ALONG DRESSING ROOMS
As Mary and Jack are talking, the door of another room opens and the head of Buster Billings comes out. He sees Jack and shouts to him to hurry up and get dressed. Jack, with another hesitating look at Mary during which he seems desirous of saying something else, turns suddenly and leaves her. She pauses a moment and looks after him. Then with a smile, she enters her own room and closes the door.
NOTE: Playing a romantic scene in blackface may be something of an experiment and very likely an unsuccessful one. As an alternative, should it not prove as effective as desired, there could be a scene after No. 161 in Jack's dressing room, showing him enter in blackface and start taking off the make-up.

160. INT. JACK'S ROOM
He enters, followed by Buster, who is urging him to get cleaned up and dressed. Jack turns to the table, hesitates, and turns around to Buster.

161. CLOSE-UP   BOTH
Jack tells him of Mary's good fortune. Buster nods understandingly as though to convey that he always knew she would "make it." Buster looks at Jack as though to read his thoughts. Then he puts an arm on Jack's shoulder and says:

TITLE 57: "Better forget it, kid. She's wrapped up in her career—and you got a chance for Broadway yourself if you keep up your present gait."

Jack nods and looks off into space. He slowly turns and reaches for the can of cold cream.[9]

FADE OUT

FADE IN

162. LONG SHOT   MICHIGAN AVENUE
It is a general atmospheric shot showing the traffic on the boulevard and the stately line of high buildings on the West Side.

163. MED. SHOT   THEATER ENTRANCE
It is the entrance to a place like Orchestra Hall. There is a placard on an easel in the center of the lobby.

164. CLOSE SHOT   ENTRANCE
The lettering on the placard is as follows:

SPECIAL MATINEE
LAST CHICAGO CONCERT
CANTOR ROSENBLATT
IN SACRED SONGS
Popular Prices

165. MED. SHOT   ENTRANCE
Among the people passing are Jack and Buster. Jack's eyes fall on the placard and he stops. Buster stops and looks at Jack, who immediately shifts his glance. He takes a quick look at his wristwatch.

166. CLOSE-UP   JACK AND BUSTER
Jack tells Buster to go ahead adding:

TITLE 58:   "Forgot something. Run along and I'll meet you at the hotel."

Buster gives him a wise look, shrugs his shoulders, and starts ahead. Jack turns as though to retrace his steps; then as he sees that Buster has vanished he darts into the theater lobby.

167. MED. SHOT   LOBBY
Jack dashes up to the box office, lays down a bill, takes a

ticket in return, and goes quickly to the entrance through which he disappears.

DISSOLVE INTO:

168.   INT. THEATER   FULL SHOT FROM CENTER
The place is filled with a fashionable throng and a generous sprinkling of Jewish types, mostly the better, well-to-do Jews of both sexes. The stage is set for concert. There is a small orchestra of string pieces and a grand piano. A man of dignified appearance and dressed in stylish afternoon clothes comes out of the wings and faces the audience.

169.   CLOSE-UP   MAN
He announces:

TITLE 59:   "The next and last number to be sung by Cantor Rosenblatt will be the famous song, 'Eli, Eli.'"

He bows and retires.

170.   MED. SHOT   STAGE
As the announcer retires, Cantor Rosenblatt appears and takes his position. He turns to the orchestra leader who gives the signal for the orchestra to play the introduction.

171.   CLOSE-UP   CANTOR
He starts singing "Eli, Eli."

172.   CLOSE SHOT   AUDIENCE
In a small group sits Jack Robin. He is sitting up straight, his eyes fixed on the cantor in an almost hypnotic stare.

173.   MED. SHOT   STAGE
Showing the cantor singing and the orchestra playing. (Other shots as needed for Vitaphone purposes.)

174.   CLOSE-UP   JACK
He has slumped in his seat and he is listening intently, his eyes still fixed on the singer.

175.   REVERSE SHOT   CANTOR
It is a fairly close shot of the singer alone as Jack would see him from a seat well in front of the house. The figure slowly dissolves into the figure of Jack's aged father, Cantor Rabinowitz.

176.   CLOSE-UP   JACK
His eyes are half closed as he visions his aged father singing in Rosenblatt's place. He rubs a hand across his eyes slowly.

177.   CLOSE-UP   RABINOWITZ
The figure slowly dissolves into the real singer, Rosenblatt. In this shot he finishes the song. He bows and starts to exit.

178.   CLOSE SHOT   SECTION AUDIENCE
They are applauding. Jack is still under the spell of the singing and his thoughts. The people on either side of him get up and start out. He is alone, slumped down in his seat, his eyes half closed again as the scene slowly FADES OUT.[10]

FADE IN

179.   SYNAGOGUE ANTEROOM
There are about twenty Jewish boys in the room, much as they were in the early part of the story. One of the boys, Moey, goes over to the battered old piano, which, like other furniture of the room, is exactly as it was ten years ago. Moey starts to play on the piano and the boys quickly gather around him. They start to sing with him. (Vitaphone.)

180.   CLOSE-UP   MOEY
He is playing and singing "Yes, Sir, She's My Baby" with much gusto.

181. MED. SHOT   GROUP
All of the boys are singing with him.

182. EXT. SYNAGOGUE
Cantor Rabinowitz, much more feeble than when we last
saw him, is approaching the door of the room in which the
boys are singing. He pauses as he hears the strains of
unfamiliar—and, to his ears, profane—music.

183. CLOSE-UP   CANTOR
As he stops, his brow sets in a frown and his lips tighten.
He throws back his shoulders in a determined manner and
starts for the door.

184. INT. ROOM   MED. SHOT
The boys are still singing the popular song to Moey's jazzy
accompaniment.

185. FULL SHOT   ROOM   FROM PIANO
The door opens and the cantor's rigid figure appears. One
of the boys jabs Moey in the back with a whispered alarm.

186. CLOSE-UP   MOEY
As the other boy jabs him, Moey, with hardly a change in
tempo, starts playing and singing "Eli, Eli" with a very
sanctimonious expression on his face.

187. MED. SHOT   BOYS
They, with Moey, are all singing "Eli, Eli."

188. FULL SHOT   ROOM   FROM DOOR
The boys are singing the famous wailing song, as the
cantor, standing in the foreground, listens uncertainly.

189. CLOSE-UP   CANTOR
He brushes a hand across his forehead in a perplexed
manner. He is sure that the music he heard from outside

was not "Eli, Eli." Yet, he is getting old and perhaps his ears are failing as well as his sight. Maybe he has done the boys an injustice. His manner relaxes and he starts toward the boys. (Vitaphone music is still going on.)

190.   FULL SHOT   ROOM

The cantor goes over to a side of the room, hangs up his battered old derby hat, and puts on his familiar skullcap. One of the boys turns around and, just as though discovering that the cantor has entered, he tells Moey.

191.   CLOSE SHOT   MOEY AND BOYS

Moey gives an exclamation of surprise and stops playing suddenly. (Vitaphone music stops.) The boys cease singing also and, with their best synagogue manner, they start toward the cantor to extend the usual salutation. Moey goes to the other side of the piano on which there is a box. He picks up the box and goes toward the cantor.

192.   MED. SHOT   CANTOR

As Moey with the box goes up to him, the other boys fall in behind him. The cantor looks at them in a surprised way, reaches in his pocket for his glasses and puts them on, looks at Moey, and says: "Nu, what is going on yet?" Moey hands the box in the direction of the cantor and starts to say something.

193.   CLOSE-UP   MOEY AND CANTOR

Moey stammers a moment, then reaches in his pocket and, with the other hand still holding out the box, he unfolds a wrinkled slip of paper with the other, holds it up, and reads it:

TITLE 60:   "On the occasion of your sixtieth birthday, Cantor Rabinowitz, your loving choir boys wish to present you this token, with best wishes for your continued peace, prosperity, and longevity."

Back to scene. Moey stammers over the last word and, with a sigh of relief, drops the paper. The cantor looks puzzled, then a smile illumines his face as he takes the box, saying:

TITLE 61:   "That was a nice speech, Moey—I forgot it was my birthday."

Moey smiles happily and, referring to the speech, he says:

TITLE 62:   "Yes, my brother Clarence what goes to collitch, writes it for me."

Meanwhile, the cantor is opening the box. He takes out a prayer shawl, wrapped in tissue paper.

194. CLOSE-UP CANTOR
He unfolds the shawl eagerly and holds it up in pleased admiration, saying:

TITLE 63:   "It's a prayer shawl! Just what I needed!"

Back to scene. There is a tear in his eye as he beams on the boys.

195. MED. SHOT GROUP
The boys gather around him. Moey assumes an air of importance.

196. CLOSE-UP MOEY
He says, in reply to the cantor's remarks:

TITLE 64:   "Yes, it's a good one. Regular price nine bucks, but we got it for seven-ninety-eight."

197. MED. SHOT GROUP
The cantor beams on Moey again as he starts wrapping the shawl up again. He puts it in its box and places it on the piano, then turns to the boys.

198.   CLOSE-UP   CANTOR
He assumes his old familiar attitude as he addresses the youngsters, saying:

TITLE 65:   "And now we sing 'Kol Nidre' some—in a month it will be Yom Kippur and we must get it good."

199.   MED. SHOT   GROUP
The boys line up in their accustomed manner, and the cantor gives them the signal to begin singing.[11]

200.   INT. LIVING ROOM   FULL SHOT
Sara is standing at the table talking to another woman, Mrs. Rubin. She is untying a parcel and the other woman is watching her eagerly.

201.   CLOSE SHOT   BOTH
As Sara unwraps the package, she takes out a prayer shawl. She holds it up in admiration as she says:

TITLE 66:   "I couldn't think of a more nice birthday present for him."

Mrs. Rubin strokes it admiringly and nods her agreement with Sara's remark.

202.   EXT. HOME
Yudelson is coming along the street with several packages and carrying a jug of wine under his arm. He mounts the steps and rings the bell at the Rabinowitz door.

203.   CLOSE-UP   YUDELSON
He readjusts the packages which are slipping from his hold. One of the packages is seen to be a large fowl, of which the feet are protruding. He transfers the jug of wine carefully to the other hand.

204.   INT. HOME
Mrs. Rabinowitz hears the bell and starts for the door. Mrs.

Rubin starts to make a hurried exit out of the back door as though not desiring to encounter visitors in her house-dress, but is prevailed upon to remain, as Sara goes to the front door to admit Yudelson. Mrs. Rabinowitz reappears, ushering in the visitor very ceremoniously. Mrs. Rubin goes up to greet the new arrival, apologizing as she does for her attire. Yudelson walks over to the table and dumps on it his parcels with a long sigh of relief. The last thing he deposits is the jug of wine, which he sets down carefully.

205.   CLOSE-UP   GROUP
As Yudelson arranges the parcels on the table, Mrs. Rabinowitz looks askance at him, and Mrs. Rubin starts fingering the fowl. He tells Sara that it is for the cantor's birthday dinner. He picks up the long package and hands it to Sara, saying:

TITLE 67:   "The turkey is from Nathan Levy for the birthday dinner—but this from me is a fine prayer shawl for the cantor."

Sara gives Mrs. Rubin an embarrassed look. Then, thanking Yudelson, she says:

TITLE 68:   "It's awful good of you—just what the cantor needs, a new shawl."

Yudelson beams proudly as Sara edges over to Mrs. Rubin. Yudelson starts walking away.

206.   CLOSE-UP   BOTH WOMEN
Sara whispers to Mrs. Rubin:

TITLE 69:   "Now I got to exchange my present for something else again."

207.   FULL SHOT   ROOM
As Sara finishes title, Yudelson joins the women. He asks where the cantor is and Sara points to the synagogue next door. Yudelson says he'll drop in on him and exits out of the

front door, leaving it open behind him. Sara picks up the packages, then drops that containing the shawl back on the table and takes the fowl into the kitchen. Mrs. Rubin tells her she must be going, and she goes out with her. In the distance she is seen going out of the back door.

208.   EXT. STREET
Coming along the street approaching the house is Jack Robin. He is walking briskly, a leather traveling bag in one hand, a cane in the other, and a straw hat set rakishly on his head. He is wearing a well-fitting grey suit, tailored in excellent taste. People he passes stop and look at him as though they thought such a figure was out of place in this neighborhood. He looks curiously at the house in which he spent his early youth and passes up the steps.

209.   EXT. ENTRANCE   CLOSE SHOT
At the door which stands slightly ajar as Yudelson left it, Jack pauses. His light manner leaves him as he finds himself again on the threshold of his home. He hesitates as though not knowing whether to ring the bell or walk in. He finally decides on the latter and enters the house hesitatingly.[12]

210.   INT. LIVING ROOM   FULL SHOT
Sara is visible through the door into the kitchen as Jack walks into the room rather haltingly. He lays down his bag on a chair, places his stick alongside of it, and looks about to note what changes have been wrought since he left home. His attention is attracted to sounds from without. He pauses and listens.

211.   INT. CHOIR ROOM   FULL SHOT
The boys under the leadership of the cantor are singing. (Vitaphone at distance.)

212.   MED. SHOT   JACK
He recognizes the air, and a look of yearning comes into his

eyes. He brushes away a tear. Then as he spies his mother in the kitchen, he coughs to attract her attention.

213.   CLOSE-UP   MOTHER
She turns suddenly from the fowl on which she has been working. She is startled for a moment, then the look of surprise is followed by a puzzled glance at the stranger in the living room. Slowly over her face comes a realization of the identity of the visitor. With a glad cry she starts toward the other room.

214.   INT. LIVING ROOM   MED. SHOT
Jack sees his mother coming toward him and, with arms outstretched, he goes forward to greet her and in a moment they are locked in each other's arms.

215.   CLOSE-UP   MOTHER AND SON
As they kiss each other affectionately, Sara wipes the tears from her eyes. There are tears of joy in Jack's eyes too. Finally he holds her off and looks at her with a semblance of his old impudent grin. He says kiddingly:

TITLE 70:   "You don't look a day older, Mama—just like a chicken."

Sara chides him with mock solemnity.

216.   CLOSE SHOT   BOTH
Sara starts plying Jack with questions which come so fast that he is obliged to call a halt. He puts a hand gently over her mouth and says, "Listen, just a minute, Mama." He adds:

TITLE 71:   "I just got into town and I hurried right down to see you and Papa before I went to find out about my new job."

Sara looks at him questioningly. He continues:

TITLE 72:   "I got a wire to come and join a new revue show—
             it's a great chance—my name in electric lights—
             everything—no more vaudeville—me Jakie
             Rabinowitz maybe a Broadway star, Mama."

Sara looks at him, only half comprehending what he is
talking about. Finally Jack sits her down in a chair.

217.   MED. SHOT   SAME
       Jack tells her to keep quiet a moment. Then he goes to his
       bag, opens it, and extracts a small jeweler's box. He hands it
       to his mother, telling her it's a little something he picked up
       for her. She holds it a moment as she looks from Jack to the
       box. He says it's for her and to open it. She does so hesitat-
       ingly, and her eyes widen as she sees the glittering brooch
       which reposes in the plush-lined box.

218.   CLOSE-UP   MOTHER
       Her lips form the word "diamonds" in a startled manner as
       her eyes reflect the glitter of the jewel. She looks up at Jack
       and says:

TITLE 73:   "Are you sure it's for me, Jakie?"

219.   MED. SHOT   BOTH
       Jack laughs as he says of course it's for her. She shakes her
       head at this unheard of extravagance. She tells him he
       shouldn't have spent so much money for her. Jack laughs
       heartily.

220.   CLOSE-UP   JACK
       He tells her that it's nothing at all, adding:

TITLE 74:   "I got so much money, Mama, Rockefeller is jealous
             of me—and Henry Ford is always trying to borrow
             from me."

He pats her shoulder tenderly.

221. MED. SHOT BOTH
      Sara gets up and tells Jack that she will call his father. Jack
      tells her not to, that he wants to look around first. He spies
      the piano and goes over to it.

222. CLOSE-UP JACK AT PIANO
      He looks over the piano, fingers the keys appraisingly, and
      asks when they got it.

223. CLOSE-UP SARA
      She says:

TITLE 75:   "The congregation presented it to Papa last year."

224. FULL SHOT ROOM
      Sara walks over to the piano as Jack sits down and starts to
      play a jazzy tune.[13] He gets through several bars when the
      front door opens and the cantor appears. He hesitates at the
      unwonted sounds coming from his cherished piano.

225. CLOSE-UP CANTOR
      His brows knit in a deep frown as he listens a moment.
      Then he takes a resolute step forward.

226. FULL SHOT ROOM FROM DOOR
      As the cantor enters the room, he takes out his glasses and
      adjusts them. Sara sees him coming and she puts a hand on
      Jack's arm to stop him, telling him that his father has
      arrived. Jack swings around on the stool, gets up, and
      hurries over to greet his father. As Jack puts out his hand,
      the cantor makes no effort to take it. Sara hurries forward.

227. CLOSE SHOT THREE
      Jack is saying, "Why, hello, Papa!" The cantor remains
      impassive as the frown deepens. Sara goes to him and,
      pointing to Jack, says eagerly to her husband:

TITLE 76:   "Look, it's your son—he said 'Hello, Papa' to you."

Jack nods in corroboration of this news. The cantor merely stiffens.

228. CLOSE-UP   CANTOR
He glares at Jack as he demands:

TITLE 77:   "What you mean, coming in my house and playing on my piano your music from the streets—your jazz?"

229. CLOSE SHOT   GROUP
Jack is abashed at this. He hesitates and Sara rushes in and takes the blame for Jack playing. She pleads with the old man to welcome Jack, but he remains adamant. He again points a condemning finger at Jack.

230. CLOSE-UP   FATHER
He almost shouts at him:

TITLE 78:   "I taught you to sing to God—to be a cantor like your fathers. But you liked better to sing in beer halls than in the temple. You're the same now."

231. CLOSE SHOT   GROUP
Sara takes the cantor's hand and pleads with him, saying that Jack doesn't deserve such treatment. Jack assumes also a pleading attitude. Sara tells the cantor to remember that it is his birthday. At this Jack goes to his bag.

232. CLOSE-UP   JACK AT CHAIR
He is rummaging in the bag excitedly and fishes out a package. He looks up and says:

TITLE 79:   "Sure, Papa, I remembered it was your birthday. See, I brought you a present too."

He unwraps it, disclosing a prayer shawl.

233. CLOSE-UP   CANTOR AND WIFE
Sara is talking to him excitedly, telling him how wonderful that Jakie should remember all these years, his papa's birthday. The cantor is beginning to weaken under this assault. Sara leaves him for Jack.

234. MED. SHOT   ROOM
Sara goes over to Jack excitedly and takes the shawl from him. As she sees it, there is just a second's change when she sees with dismay that it is another prayer shawl. Her manner changes immediately to one of excited delight. As Jack looks appealingly at his father, Sara holds up the shawl for him.

235. CLOSE-UP   SARA
As she holds up the shawl, stroking its soft folds affectionately, she says:

TITLE 80:   "See, Papa, just what you needed—a nice new prayer shawl."

She starts toward him.

236. MED. SHOT   GROUP
Jack follows Sara to the side of the old man. He takes the shawl from her and addressing his father says, almost tearfully:

TITLE 81:   "Many happy returns of the day to our cantor. Ever hear that before when I was a little boy, Papa?"

237. CLOSE SHOT   GROUP
As the cantor stands impassively, Sara takes his arm and says to him:

TITLE 82:   "Look, Papa, Jakie is making you a speech, like when he was a little boy on your birthday."

The cantor looks up as though from a reverie and, bowing in a dignified manner, says: "Thank you." He makes no

97

effort to take the shawl, which Sara takes. She exclaims upon the fine weave and cloth, saying it is the best one the cantor has ever had, etc. Jack grows more embarrassed as the cantor shows no sign of relenting and shifts from one foot to another. He finally looks away from his father to his mother and, taking the cue from her, remarks:

TITLE 83:   "Sure, it's a good one—the best money could buy."

The old man shows interest at this. He repeats the boy's words. There is a question in his manner, or a conclusion, but seizing upon it as an opening, Jack eagerly declares:

TITLE 84:   "Sure, Papa, I'm making plenty jack. And I'm going to make more. Ain't many can put over a Mammy song like me."

He continues talking about his work. The old man's eyes assume a steely glitter. Jack continues talking glibly.

238.   CLOSE-UP   FATHER
He glares at Jack. Finally he holds up a hand for silence, then snaps out:

TITLE 85:   "So you sing your dirty songs in theayters now? First on the sidewalks, then beer halls and now theayters."

239.   CLOSE-UP   GROUP
Sara tries to stop the old man. Jack, surprised at this new attack, tries to defend himself. The old man doesn't want to listen. Finally Jack, aroused now to the fact that he must fight to get the respect of his father, demands that his father listen to him. He grasps his father's hand. The old man stares at him in surprise. He starts to protest and Jack silences him.

240.   CLOSE-UP   JACK
He leans forward as he says, earnestly:

TITLE 86: "You taught me to sing—and you told me that music was the voice of God—and it is just as honorable to sing in the theater as in the synagogue."

241. CLOSE-UP FATHER AND SON
As Jack finishes title, he endeavors to continue but the old man stops him. He points to the door. Jack, with a gesture of defeat, turns away from him, toward the chair upon which are his things.

242. MED. SHOT GROUP
Sara goes to the old man and pleads with him not to be so hard on their only boy. The old man stiffens and waves her away. Jack starts closing his bag. The old man picks up the shawl and holds it to him, saying that he wants nothing bought with his unclean money.

Jack disregards him, closing the bag. Sara takes it and the old man tells her to burn it if it is not taken away. Jack turns to his mother. She comes to him, and he puts his arms around her. The old man stands like a statue waiting for Jack to leave his roof. Sara kisses Jack, and he kisses her and pats her on the back.

243. CLOSE-UP JACK AND MOTHER
He finally disengages her hands and talks to her soothingly. He picks up his things and starts to go. Then he turns and faces his father.

244. CLOSE-UP FATHER
He stands looking over Jack's head, silently waiting his departure.

245. CLOSE-UP JACK
He hesitates a moment, then addresses his father quietly. He says:

TITLE 87: "Some day, Papa, maybe you'll understand things like Mama does."

246. MED. SHOT   GROUP

The father affects not to hear. He merely points to the door. Jack turns to his mother, says good-by to her again, and starts toward the door. The old man stands impassively as Jack passes him on his way out. Sara makes an impulsive gesture in Jack's direction, but the old man stays her with a slight movement of his hand.

SLOW FADE OUT

FADE IN

247. FULL SHOT   STAGE THEATER

The camera is set upstage center and is shooting toward footlights. There is a row of twenty-four chorus girls downstage, extending across, all in rehearsal rompers, and they are dancing in unison. As they finish a kick, a tall lanky figure of a man in shirt-sleeves rises from the footlights and halts them with a hand in the air. He is Jim Sparks who puts on the dances, and he starts telling the girls in expressive language just what he thinks of their efforts and where he thinks they belong.

248. CLOSE-UP   SPARKS

He finishes telling them what he thinks of them, then tells them to watch him. Although his timing and technique are correct, his efforts, because of his build and attire, make him appear ludicrous. He stops and calls to the piano player to do it over again. Addressing the girls, he says:

TITLE 88:   "Now let's have some life in it—and don't be afraid of busting anything."

249. FULL SHOT   STAGE FROM SIDE

Sparks backs away and the girls go into the steps as he did it. He nods approvingly. A small group of people appear in the wings on the opposite side of the stage and stand watching the dancers. There are two men and a woman.

250.　CLOSE SHOT　GROUP

Camera is in wings behind them and dancers are seen in the background going through their evolutions. The girl turns to talk to the man at her left, and it is seen that she is Mary Dale. The man is Randolph Dillings, a middle-aged, well-dressed, rather distinguished type, a well-to-do businessman who finds amusement and sometimes profit in dabbling in stage enterprises. The other man, somewhat younger, is Harry Lee, the producer of the show.

251.　CLOSE-UP　DILLINGS

He looks away from the dancers and says something to Lee.

TITLE 89:　　Randolph Dillings whose money was behind the new edition of "April Follies."

Back. He is talking.

252.　CLOSE-UP　LEE

He answers Dillings and turns away with a frown.

TITLE 90:　　Harry Lee who was staking his reputation as a producer on the same show.

He is watching the girls and nervously chewing his cigar. He takes out his watch and looks at it.

253.　CLOSE SHOT　THREE

Lee turns to Mary and tells her that it is about time that the new comedian is showing up. Mary smiles and tells him that they needn't worry about him. Dillings turns to Mary anxiously and says:

TITLE 91:　　"You're sure, Mary, that this discovery of yours can sing as well as Hal Bolton?"

Mary nods and smiles confidently. She says:

TITLE 92:　　"He's better than Bolton. You won't be sorry you took my advice." [14]

The men continue to look worried, however, and Mary starts to tell them more about the new comedian.

254.   EXT. STAGE DOOR
The old man who sits in the doorway looks up and instinctively puts a foot across the entrance, and a second later Jack Robin appears. He is not carrying the bag or cane now. Otherwise he appears as he did a few hours earlier at the home of his father. He tells the old man who he is. The latter grudgingly admits him.

255.   FULL SHOT   STAGE FROM WINGS
The three are still in the foreground, and Sparks is drilling the girls on the stage relentlessly. They stop at the end of the dance, and Sparks walks over to the group. Dillings steps over and starts to talk to him as Jack comes into the scene. Mary turns as she hears his step and goes to greet him. Lee stands where he was. Jack stops as he sees Mary. She goes to him with outstretched hands.

256.   CLOSE-UP   JACK AND MARY
He stands looking at Mary in a surprised manner as she comes into scene and greets him. Jack is still speechless except for the first "Mary Dale!" Mary takes his hand. He looks at her, then blurts out:

TITLE   93:   "Why, what are you doing here?"

Mary laughs mischievously as she asks him if he has any objections to her being there. Jack in an embarrassed manner says that he only said that because he was so surprised to see her. He says:

TITLE   94:   "Then you're in this show, too?"

Mary nods and says with mock modesty:

TITLE   95:   "I'm merely the star, sir."

She looks up at him and says with a smile:

TITLE 96:   "And you're to be the other star."

Jack looks at her in a stunned manner. Gradually he solves the riddle: it was Mary who was responsible for his summons to the big city—the great chance at last to shine on Broadway, every actor's ultimate goal. He starts to blurt out his thanks. Mary stops him, then with a hurried look around, she tells him to wait until later and they'll talk it all over.

257.   MED. SHOT   SAME
Lee and Dillings come into the scene and Mary presents Jack to them. Jack is somewhat embarrassed. He shakes hands perfunctorily with Dillings but is rather more impressed by Lee. Dillings turns away after the introduction, and Lee, trying to put Jack at his ease, asks him if he will be ready for a rehearsal that evening. Jack nods.

258.   CLOSE-UP   JACK AND LEE
Lee takes a part book out of his pocket and hands it to Jack and tells him he will give him the songs later. He says to Jack:

TITLE 97:   "You've been very highly recommended—but we've only got one person's word for it that you can deliver."

Jack takes a step closer to Lee eagerly and tells him that he is sure that he can make good. Lee nods rather ruefully and says:

TITLE 98:   "Well if you don't I'm sunk, because there is only two weeks before the opening—and Dillings will be out a bunch of jack."

Back to scene. Jack again assures him eagerly.

259.   MED. SHOT   GROUP
Mary and Dillings rejoin Jack and Lee. Mary's attitude toward Jack is so friendly that Dillings looks askance at her.

Mary and Jack start talking about the last time they saw each other in Chicago. Dillings breaks in on the conversation. Lee looks at his watch and walks away toward the center of the stage.

260.   CLOSE SHOT   THREE

Dillings turns to Mary and says that if she is ready he will take her to dinner. Mary hesitates a moment, then after a quick look at Jack, she turns to Dillings and says:

TITLE   99:   "I'm awfully sorry—I just promised Mr. Robin I'd have dinner with him—I want to tell him about the play."

Dillings looks from one to the other and, with an inarticulate grunt of disgust, he raises his hat grudgingly and stalks out of the scene. Jack stands looking at Mary dumbly. She turns and smiles at him.

LAP DISSOLVE INTO:

261.   INT. CAFE   CLOSE-UP

Jack and Mary are sitting in a corner of the cafe at a little table facing each other. Mary is talking with animation. The waiter sets down some dishes before them and exits. Mary finishes what she is saying and Jack leans forward. He says:

TITLE   100:   "I can never—if I live to be a million—ever thank you, Mary, for what you have done for me."

Mary holds up a hand in mock severity, much in the attitude of a traffic cop halting an auto. She tells him to forget it. He says that he can't and doesn't want to forget it. She is becoming embarrassed under his earnestness. Finally he reaches over and takes her hand. Her eyes look away from him. He leans over further and says half whisperingly:

TITLE   101:   "I suppose you think I'm out of my head, but I—I'm crazy about you, Mary."

Mary looks up and says promptly:

TITLE 102:   "I'm crazy about you, too."

Jack looks at her then, a puzzled imploring look. He stammers out:

TITLE 103:   "You don't know what I mean."

Mary smiles and says, "What do you mean?" Jack takes a deep breath and blurts out:

TITLE 104:   "I mean that I love you—that I want to marry you."

Mary leans over. The smile leaves her face. She strokes his hand as she says quietly:

TITLE 105:   "That is what I thought you meant."

They lean over closely, looking into each other's eyes.

FADE OUT

FADE IN

262.   CLOSE-UP   DILLINGS

The camera is behind him and takes in part of his shoulder and hand holding newspaper, without disclosing his identity.

DISSOLVE INTO:

Vignetted column section which reads as follows:

INSERT NEWSPAPER

"April Follies," which will be the next musical revue on Broadway, opens tomorrow night at the Fulton with several newcomers making their bow in New York. Heading the list will be Jack Robin, recruited from vaudeville, who is expected to prove a sensation, and Mary Dale, the clever danseuse, a vaudeville headliner early this season. Robin is said to have been discovered by Miss Dale while singing in a resort in San Francisco.

DISSOLVE INTO:

263.   CLOSE-UP   DILLINGS FROM FRONT

He is seated in a very luxuriously equipped office. He

shows much annoyance at what he has read. He crumples up the paper and throws it on the floor. Then he hurls his cigar into a corner of the room. He pauses a moment as though considering what to do and finally jumps to his feet.

264. FULL SHOT   OFFICE
Dillings goes quickly over to a hat tree, takes his coat and hat, and exits hastily.

265. INT. THEATER
With camera in fly gallery, unique shot may be had of chorus in action on stage in the midst of a rehearsal. Mary Dale is doing her dance with the chorus.

266. CLOSE-UP   MARY
She is seen as from the front in her dance.

267. FULL SHOT   STAGE FROM WINGS
The chorus closes in behind Mary in some evolution of the dance, as Jack and another player, both in costume, come into the foreground. As the dance ends, they applaud heartily, and Lee, who has taken charge of the last few rehearsals, motions from the side, dismissing them. The girls troop off on the other side and Mary comes over to Jack.

268. CLOSE-UP   JACK AND MARY
Jack is still applauding Mary as she, slightly out of breath from her exertions, joins him. He takes her hands and tells her what a wonderful dancer she is. Mary smiles in a deprecating manner and says:

TITLE 106:   "But it's *you* who will be famous tomorrow night, Jack. It looks very much as though it were *your* show. They're giving you everything."

Jack makes a nervous, self-disparaging gesture. Then he comes closer to her and says:

TITLE 107: "If I'm the success all of you think I will be, I will only have you to thank."

Mary smiles and, without saying anything further, she presses his hand and starts out of the scene toward her dressing room.

269. FULL SHOT STAGE
As Mary leaves him, Jack turns around to look after her. He hesitates, however, as he sees Lee and Randolph Dillings, a few steps away, follow the girl with their eyes, then turn and look at him. Jack starts toward them, then, seeing that they start talking earnestly together, he turns the other way as though to go over on the other side of the stage. He goes to the piano downstage.

270. CLOSE-UP LEE AND DILLINGS
Dillings has finished saying something to him as Lee's jaw drops. He looks at him in surprise and blurts out:

TITLE 108: "You don't mean you'd take your money out of the show the last minute?"

Back to scene. Dillings nods firmly. Lee demands to know the reason for this sudden determination. Dillings points in the direction of Mary's room and then to Jack. He says:

TITLE 109: "Just the idea of Mary's interest in this jazz singer of yours."

Back to scene. Lee starts to argue with Dillings, telling him that it is nothing serious. Dillings, however, has guessed the true state of affairs. He adds:

TITLE 110: "I have no further interest in her career. Just mail me a check today."

He starts to leave.

271. FULL SHOT STAGE
As Dillings leaves, Lee follows him, still eagerly trying to

explain that there is nothing between the two principals of the show. Just as he is about to exit, Mary comes from her dressing room and almost collides with him. Lee rushes up to them and takes Dillings's arm. Jack, who is at the piano, sees Mary and starts across stage toward the group.

272.   MED. SHOT   GROUP
Mary takes Dillings's arm, and he stops his progress somewhat unwillingly. It is evident that he wishes to avoid a scene with Mary. Before she can say anything, however, Lee says to Mary:

TITLE 111:   "He's taking his money out of the show on account of Jack."

Dillings is growing more embarrassed. Mary looks at Lee, then at Dillings, not understanding at first. Then she realizes the true situation. She looks at Lee.

273.   CLOSE-UP   MARY AND LEE
She smiles quietly and says to Lee:

TITLE 112:   "I suppose you would like to have me say that I only regard Jack as a fellow performer."

Lee nods eagerly. The smile does not leave Mary's face. She turns away from Lee.

274.   CLOSE-UP   OF THREE
As Lee leans closer to hear her answer, Mary says to Dillings:

TITLE 113:   "Well, I'm sorry that I cannot—or perhaps it would be better to say that I am glad."

Dillings nods in quiet acquiescence. Lee looks crestfallen. Mary puts a hand affectionately on Lee's arm.

275.   MED. SHOT   GROUP
Dillings is raising his hat as he endeavors again to leave, just as Jack comes into the scene. Jack goes up to Dillings

and says "how do you do" to him. The latter gives him a
cold look of nonrecognition, bows again stiffly to the other
two, and exits, Jack looking after him in mock dismay.

276. CLOSE-UP JACK
He looks at the other two and says ruefully:

TITLE 114:   "I just got a hunch that he don't like me—maybe he
thinks I wear these clothes on the street."

He looks down at his trick suit.

277. CLOSE SHOT   THREE
Mary and Lee laugh at this sally, and as Jack joins them,
Mary looks up at Lee, her hand on his arm:

278. CLOSE-UP MARY
She says to Lee:

TITLE 115:   "Does it mean that you are going to be in a fix for
money?"

279. CLOSE-UP   THREE
Lee pats the girl's hand. He hesitates, then says, "Oh, I'm
always in a fix for money." Mary is too much in earnest,
however, to accept this light dismissal of his difficulty. She
looks up at him and says:

TITLE 116:   "If you need it, Mr. Lee, I have a few thousand in
the savings bank, and—"

Lee stops her, telling her that she is a good kid and how
much he appreciates her offer, but he'll worry through all
right. Jack is about to say something, when the stage doorkeeper enters and addresses him. Lee mops his brow in his
nervousness and starts away from group. Mary looks after
him, reflecting his worry.[15]

280. CLOSE-UP JACK AND DOORMAN
He is telling Jack that there is a caller for him. Jack asks
again what the name is. The doorman says:

TITLE 117:   "Says his name is Bugelson, or something like that,
and he knew you when . . . "

Jack breaks in on him, his face lighting up. He tells the
doorkeeper to show the man in. The doorman leaves.[16]

281.   FULL SHOT   STAGE
The chorus girls are trooping out on the stage from all sides
for another number when Yudelson is seen entering from
the outer entrance. He looks around puzzled, as he would
be on a first visit to such a place. He stops and looks around
him, puzzled by the strange surroundings.

282.   CLOSE-UP   YUDELSON
He is dressed in his best *Shabbas* suit as befits the business
head of a prosperous congregation as well as a successful
broker. He looks around in a dazed way and his eyes fall on
the girls of the chorus. He has never seen that many bare
knees in his life and his eyes bulge. He starts in the direction of the stage where the girls are congregating, in the
manner of a man under a hypnotic spell.

283.   MED. SHOT   JACK
Jack, who has been talking to Mary, spies Yudelson and
starts toward him. Mary goes to the stage opening.

284.   CLOSE-UP   GROUP OF GIRLS
One of the girls in the center of the group is doing some
high kicks and the others are critically viewing her efforts.

285.   MED. SHOT   STAGE
Yudelson walks right out on the stage where the girls are
grouped, his eyes fixed on the kicker's legs. Jack comes up
to him and takes his arm, and Yudelson comes out of his
trance.

286.   CLOSE-UP   YUDELSON AND JACK
Yudelson exclaims with pleasure as Jack takes his hand and

shakes it, although he is still puzzled at Jack's appearance. He shakes his head as he sees the changes that the years have wrought in the boy. He points to the door and says:

TITLE 118:   "He didn't know who I mean by Jake Rabino-witz—I forget your mama told me you are now Jakie Robin."

Jack laughs and takes Yudelson's arm to walk him off the stage.

287.   FULL SHOT   STAGE
As Jack and Yudelson walk toward camera, Lee calls for the rehearsal of another number and the girls start taking their positions. Yudelson, now in the immediate foreground, turns around to get another look. Jack, laughing, turns him back the other way, telling him that he's liable to lose an eye if he doesn't look out. Yudelson pulls himself together. He turns to Jack seriously as both stop just clear of the stage.

288.   CLOSE-UP   BOTH
Yudelson tells Jack he has an important message for him. Jack looks at him, a question in his eyes. Yudelson says:

TITLE 119:   "Tomorrow it is Yom Kippur and we want you should sing 'Kol Nidre' in the temple."

Jack looks at him in astonishment as Yudelson keeps talking about the meeting of the committee and how he had held out for Jack, who looks at him in surprise. He tries to interrupt several times but Yudelson rattles on. Finally Jack takes his arm and stops him, asking what it's all about. He says:

TITLE 120:   "But what's the matter with my father singing, Mr. Yudelson?"

Yudelson looks surprised, then says: "I forgot to tell you, your papa is sick." Jack is alarmed at this. He asks how long he has been sick and if his illness is serious. Yudelson says:

TITLE 121: "It's been two weeks—since the day you was there—and he's got a good doctor—Dr. O'Shaughnessy from the Rockefeller Institute."

Jack looks thoughtful.

289. CLOSE-UP   JACK
He is saying to himself: "Two weeks—since the day I was there."

290. CLOSE-UP   BOTH
Jack looks at Yudelson as though weighing his request. Yudelson continues with his arguments, saying that some of the committee were against it, but he insisted because they all owed him money. As a final argument he says to Jack, eagerly:

TITLE 122: "It would be a fine surprise for your papa if you sing."

Jack shakes his head slowly. He says, "But he threw me out of the house only two weeks ago." Yudelson nods and replies:

TITLE 123: "Sure, he threw you out but a son's a son no matter if he is thrown out twenty times by his papa."

Back to scene. Jack smiles at Yudelson's eagerness to overcome his objections. He looks toward the stage, then turns to the old man, shaking his head as he says, with an air of finality:

TITLE 124: "But, Mr. Yudelson, our show opens tomorrow night—it's the chance I've dreamed of for years—I can't do what you ask."

Yudelson shrugs his shoulders hopelessly and starts to turn.

291. MED. SHOT   SAME
As Yudelson turns, Mary comes into scene. Yudelson

pauses and looks at her. Jack, somewhat embarrassed as Mary looks from him to Yudelson, introduces them. Yudelson gives her an admiring look. He gives Jack a look of approval as though personally complimenting him on his good taste. Realizing instinctively that the girl has some influence with Jack, he tries to prevail on her to persuade Jack to do what he wants.

292. CLOSE-UP   THREE
Mary looks at Yudelson, then at Jack. The latter explains the situation. Mary looks at Yudelson, full of sympathy but unable to help him. She shakes her head as she tells him the impossibility of his wish coming true. Yudelson shakes hands with Jack, then with Mary and turns to leave.

293. MED. SHOT   SAME
As Yudelson walks slowly away, Lee comes into the scene. He pauses and looks toward the stage.

294. CLOSE-UP   LEE
He yells to the girls:

TITLE 125:   "Remember, dress rehearsal at two tomorrow— and I don't want anyone drifting in at five after two."

He turns to the others.

295. CLOSE-UP   JACK AND MARY
Jack is on the verge of tears and Mary pats his shoulder softly.

                                        FADE OUT

FADE IN
296. LIVING ROOM   CANTOR'S HOME
Yudelson is sitting in a rocking chair reading a Yiddish newspaper. Mrs. Rubin is using a broom on the floor. She comes over to Yudelson and starts to talk with him.

297.   CLOSE-UP   BOTH
The woman points to the bedroom door and asks Yudelson if he thinks the cantor will recover. Yudelson affects a facetious manner in order to cover up his grief. He says, flippantly:

TITLE 126:   "Am I a doctor or a riddle guesser you should ask me such questions? I am worrying now about who sings 'Kol Nidre' when Yom Kippur begins tonight."

298.   MED. SHOT   SAME
Mrs. Rubin shakes her head sadly and continues her work. Seeing that he is not observed, Yudelson takes out his handkerchief surreptitiously and gives his eyes a furtive wipe. He looks toward the bedroom door in the background as it opens, and a young woman in nurse's garb comes into the room. Yudelson gets up and rushes to her with a question as to how the cantor is getting along. She shakes her head, and Yudelson drops into the chair as the nurse proceeds to the kitchen.

299.   INT. BEDROOM   FULL SHOT
Cantor Rabinowitz, pale and emaciated, is lying helplessly on the bed. His eyes are open and are fixed on the figure of Sara who is busying herself about the room. He motions feebly to her, and she hastens over to his side. She sits in the chair at the bedside and leans over closely to hear what he has to say, gently stroking his hand which she has taken.

300.   CLOSE-UP   CANTOR AND WIFE
He asks her to lean closer and as she does he starts to whisper to her.

301.   CLOSE-UP   CANTOR
He looks at his wife pathetically. He says hesitatingly:

TITLE 127:   "It's Yom Kippur tonight—the first time in forty-five years I didn't sing in the temple."

302.   CLOSE-UP   BOTH
Sara pats his hand soothingly and tells him not to worry
about that—that he will be well sooner if he doesn't worry.
His eyes are in the past, however, and he is not listening to
her. He continues:

TITLE 128:   "It will be the first time in five generations a
Rabinowitz has not sung on the Day of Atone-
ment."

He closes his eyes as he says this and is silent for awhile.
Sara continues stroking his hand.

303.   MED. SHOT   LIVING ROOM
Mrs. Rubin is again talking to Yudelson. He is trying to get
her to quit talking.

304.   CLOSE-UP   BOTH
She leans over and, undismayed by his manner, she asks
with many gestures:

TITLE 129:   "But who will sing tonight in the cantor's place?"

Yudelson makes a gesture of repulsion. He waves her away
with:

TITLE 130:   "You should let me worry about that—*I* am the
chairman."

He tries to read again. She asks him why they don't get
Jakie back. He ignores her and says:

TITLE 131:   "Anyhow, it won't be that croaker Levy who will
sing."

305.   FULL SHOT   ROOM
Mrs. Rubin hears a ring at the door and hurries to the
entrance. Yudelson gets up as Dr. O'Shaughnessy enters.
He is a big husky, grey-haired Irishman, and he greets the
two of them heartily, as one would very old friends.

306.   INT. BEDROOM   CLOSE-UP
The cantor still has his eyes closed, and Sara is stroking his forehead. Without opening his eyes, he reaches up and puts his withered old hand on that of hers. He opens his eyes and smiles wanly at her. Then he says:

TITLE 132:   "I been dreaming Jakie came back to sing 'Kol Nidre'—"

307.   CLOSE-UP   CANTOR
He pauses a moment, then continues:

TITLE 133:   "Maybe God would forgive him—if he would come tonight and sing."

He closes his eyes.

308.   CLOSE-UP   BOTH
Sara looks startled as the idea comes into her mind of getting Jakie. She removes her hand and looks down to measure the possible effect of her departure.

309.   FULL SHOT   ROOM
As Sara is nervously considering her next step, the door opens and the doctor enters, solving Sara's problem for the moment. She tells the cantor that the doctor is here and that she will go away for a little while. The nurse follows the doctor into the room and Sara exits.

310.   INT. LIVING ROOM
As Sara enters, she goes hurriedly to Yudelson. Mrs. Rubin comes over hastily in fear of losing a word.

311.   CLOSE-UP   GROUP
Sara tells Yudelson that she is going to get Jakie. The latter tells her it's no use, but she is insistent, and he agrees to go along. Sara tells Mrs. Rubin to remain there until they return.[17]

312.   INT. BEDROOM   MED. SHOT

The doctor is leaning over the sick man, listening to his heart with a stethoscope. The cantor's eyes are closed. The nurse stands at the side of the doctor. He raises up, folds the stethoscope, and looks at the nurse. They exchange a look which both understand as leaving little hope for the life of the cantor.

FADE OUT

FADE IN

313.   THEATER STAGE FROM FRONT

The orchestra is in the foreground, and the curtain is down. In the immediate foreground are empty seats in the first few rows of the house, and several men with hats on are sitting down front. Lee is among them. He calls out something, and the orchestra starts to play the curtain music. (This may be Vitaphoned with good effect.)

314.   CLOSE-UP   LEE AND OTHER MAN

The man with him is a typical businessman of Hebraic type—the sort that one finds financing shows on Broadway. Lee turns to him and says:

TITLE   134:   "A dress rehearsal isn't the easiest thing on the nerves."

The other man nods sympathetically. He replies:

TITLE   135:   "If that new jazz singer is what you say he is— we've got nothing to worry about."

315.   FULL SHOT   STAGE FROM FRONT

The men are in the foreground as before, and Lee nods anxiously as the other man finishes the title. The orchestra gives a signal and the curtain goes up, showing the line of girls across the stage for their first number. (This should be Vitaphoned and the volume cut down to a minimum when we cut to the following scenes in the dressing room.)

316. INT. JACK'S DRESSING ROOM
Jack is dressed and is just beginning to put on his facial
make-up when Mary enters. She pirouettes before him and
pouts as he evinces only a slight interest in her. She stops
and goes over to him.

317. CLOSE-UP   JACK AND MARY
Mary puts a hand on Jack's shoulder and, pointing to her
costume, as he turns around, says to him:

TITLE 136:   "You haven't said a word about my nice new costume for the first dance."

Back. Jack gives himself a mental dig and assumes an air of
much interest. Mary, however, has lost her interest in Jack's
reactions to her appearance by this time. She realizes that
Jack is worried about his father. She asks him if that is what
is worrying him. Jack shakes his head. He says:

TITLE 137:   "No, I have only one thing on my mind now—the
opening tonight."

He turns to his make-up. Mary shakes her head. She knows
that the other matter is worrying him more than that. Jack
starts to blacken his face.

318. LONG SHOT   STAGE
This is a shot downward from fly gallery, showing one of
the ensemble dance numbers in progress, just as it would
be were the performance really on. The chorus falls back
and two adagio dancers come on.

319. MED. SHOT   STAGE FROM FRONT
The adagio dancers do a part of their routine.

320. CLOSE-UP   DRESSING ROOM
Jack has just about completed his make-up. Mary is sitting
on a chair a short distance away. They are talking as Jack
puts the finishing touches to his make-up, the enlarging of
the lips. Mary leans over.

321. CLOSE-UP BOTH
Mary asks him just what Yudelson wanted of him. Jack explains about the age-old customs, which mark the observation of Yom Kippur. Mary nods as he explains. She says:

TITLE 138: "And they want you to sing tonight in his place?"

Back. Jack nods. He throws out his hands in an eloquent gesture as he tells her how hopeless it is. He adds as he leans over earnestly:

TITLE 139: "I don't really belong there—here's where I belong, on Broadway, but there's something in the blood that sort of calls you—something apart from this life."

Mary nods understandingly. She says:

TITLE 140: "I think I understand, Jack. But no matter how strong the call, this is your life."

322. MED. SHOT SAME
Jack nods and gets up. He inspects his make-up in the glass closely. Mary looks at herself in the long glass at the other side of the room as the stage doortender enters. He pauses in the door and, as Jack sees him, he tells Jack that there is someone at the door to see him.

323. CLOSE-UP DOORTENDER
He says apologetically:

TITLE 141: "It's the old bird who was here yesterday—and he's got a lady with him." [18]

324. FULL SHOT ROOM
Jack stands and stares at him. Mary starts for the door saying that she will leave. Jack motions to her to remain.

325. LONG SHOT TOWARD DOOR
Before the old doorman can turn, Yudelson enters, followed by Sara. She is wearing a shawl over her housedress, just as

she left in her haste. As Jack sees her he goes rapidly toward her, crying, "Mama!" She stands and looks at him in a puzzled way. He goes up and takes her hands in his. He starts to kiss her, then remembers her [*sic*] make-up. Sara holds him off as Yudelson comes up to them, looking at Jack in a puzzled manner.

326. CLOSE-UP THREE
Sara looks at Jack, eager though puzzled, and says:

TITLE 142:   "Jakie, this ain't you . . . "

Yudelson adds:

TITLE 143:   "It talks like Jakie, but it looks like a nigger."

Sara waves Yudelson aside, telling Jack that she has something to ask him. Jack asks her to sit down, and he sits down opposite her. She starts pouring out her grief in an uninterrupted flow of words.

327. FULL SHOT ROOM
Mary is standing in the doorway, in the foreground. She looks intently from the mother to her son, her gaze resting on him to see, if possible, what the results of this visit will be. Then she turns slowly and leaves them, a worried frown on her face.

328. CLOSE-UP MOTHER AND SON
He is leaning close as she talks. He tries to interrupt her with a hopeless gesture, but she motions to him to listen to her. She continues:

TITLE 144:   "For generations God has heard a Rabinowitz sing every Day of Atonement . . . God is used to it . . . "

She pauses for a breath and adds:

TITLE 145:   "Maybe your papa is dying. God will ask him— and he will have to tell him his only son is singing in a theayter instead . . . "

She leans over closer and pleads with him.

329. CLOSE-UP   YUDELSON
He leans over and adds his argument:

TITLE 146:   "And if you don't come, there is only Levy the
              Shammas to sing—with a voice like a frog."

He gives a gesture of disgust.

330. CLOSE-UP   MOTHER AND SON
Jack takes her hand tenderly and tells her that what she asks
is impossible, that they're all depending on him—that this
is the one big chance of his life. Fame and fortune will be
his if he succeeds. He adds:

TITLE 147:   "And that's what you are asking me to give up."

He gives her a pleading look.

331. FULL SHOT   ROOM
Gene, the stage manager, comes to the door and summons
Jack. He starts to get up and Sara clings to him. Mary enters
again, worried about Jack.

332. CLOSE-UP   GENE
He says to Jack that the orchestra is already playing his
introduction.

333. CLOSE-UP   JACK AND MOTHER
He unfastens her hands gently from him. He tells her that
he must go on the stage and tells her to wait.

334. MED. SHOT   ROOM
Jack starts out of the room with his mother's last plea
ringing in his ears. Mary goes to her and puts her arm
around her. Yudelson follows Jack out curiously.

335. FULL SHOT   STAGE FROM FRONT
The chorus is lined up looking toward entrance at which

Jack is expected. The orchestra is playing the introduction to his song as he enters. He speaks the few lines which serve as an introduction to his song and then begins singing it.

NOTE: The rendition of the song will have to be governed entirely by the Vitaphone routine decided upon. The scenes herewith are only those necessary to carrying on the story. In all scenes before he exits, the voice of Jack is heard in volume according to the distance from him.

336.   CLOSE-UP   JACK
He goes into the first bars of his song.

337.   MED. SHOT   OUTSIDE ROOM
Yudelson and Sara are watching through the wings, but back in the passage leading to the outside door. Mary asks Mrs. Rabinowitz if she doesn't want to go closer. She points to the stage but the mother shakes her head.

338.   CLOSE-UP   YUDELSON
He is listening, an ear cocked stageward. He nods as he says, half to himself:

TITLE 148:   "Yes, that's Jakie—with the cry in the voice, just like in the temple."

He looks away hurriedly.

339.   MED. SHOT   YUDELSON
Two girls in very scant attire make him forget Jack for the moment as they pass close to him. He looks after them in a daze and starts to follow them.

340.   FULL SHOT   PASSAGE
Mary still has an arm around Sara. The latter, overcome by emotion, starts for the door. Mary tries to hold her because of Jack.

341. CLOSE-UP   BOTH

As Mary endeavors to persuade Sara to remain, Sara tearfully says that she must go. She turns to Mary and says,
hopelessly:

TITLE 149:   "Here he belongs—If God wanted him in His
house, He would have kept him there."

Mary nods understandingly. Sara starts for the door.

342. FULL SHOT   SAME

Mary starts with Sara. Yudelson suddenly sees them going
toward the door. He looks after the two girls who had
attracted his attention, as though not knowing which to
follow, then reluctantly follows Sara. In the doorway Mary
leans over and kisses Sara. The latter grasps the girl's arms
eagerly.

343. CLOSE-UP   MARY AND SARA

The mother says to her:

TITLE 150:   "Tell him maybe he can see his papa anyhow before it is too late."

Mary nods and Sara exits. Mary looks after her sorrowfully.

344. MED. SHOT   STAGE

Jack is singing.

345. CLOSE-UP   LEE AND GENE

They are standing in the wings. They look at each other in
speechless admiration of Jack's singing.

346. LONG SHOT   THROUGH WINGS

Jack finishes song and makes exit. As he comes into foreground, he is surrounded by Lee, Gene, Mary, and several
of the other principals. They grab his hands and congratu-
late him. He smiles gratefully.

347. CLOSE-UP   JACK AND LEE
The latter is enthusiastically pumping Jack's hand as he says:

TITLE 151:   "Wonderful, Jack!! You were actually crying. Do it that way tonight and you're a hit on Broadway!"

He drops Jack's hands and turns to Gene with instructions for the next act.

348. MED. SHOT   OUTSIDE DRESSING ROOM
Those surrounding Jack fall away from him as Mary goes to him. She takes his hand and shakes it. She pantomimes that his mother has gone. Then she turns and leaves. Jack wipes a white glove across his eyes, leaving a white streak on his damp face. He comes slowly toward the camera and enters the door of his dressing room.

349. MED. SHOT   ROOM
Jack goes slowly to one of the chairs in the room, drops heavily into it, and then leans over and puts his blackened face into the white gloves.

                                        SLOW FADE OUT

FADE IN
350. CHOIR ROOM SYNAGOGUE
Yudelson is presiding at a meeting of the synagogue trustees. He is seated at the head of the little cheap table with a very important air. There are four others, all in their holiday clothes. One is Levy, the *Shammas*, or sexton, a little scrawny fellow with a straggling beard. Two others have the long orthodox beards, and the fifth member of the committee is clean-shaven, a prosperous Jewish businessman. Yudelson says something and they all start talking at once. Levy finally attracts the attention of Yudelson. He gets up and tries to speak. Yudelson endeavors to quiet him, but Levy is insistent.

351. CLOSE-UP   LEVY
He holds out both hands pleadingly, as he says:

TITLE 152:   "Gentlemen, I think it should be *me* who should
sing in the cantor's place. I—"

352. CLOSE SHOT   TABLE
Yudelson interrupts him, pounding on the table and or-
dering him to sit down. He insists that he is chairman and
must be listened to.

353. CLOSE-UP   YUDELSON
He yells out at Levy:

TITLE 153:   "Do you think, schlemiel, our congregation paid
for special music to hear you squawking like a
tomcat yet?"

He glares at Levy.

354. CLOSE SHOT   GROUP
Levy subsides with a beaten gesture. His lifelong wish to
sing "Kol Nidre" has been dashed to the ground. Yudelson
continues rubbing it in.

355. CLOSE-UP   YUDELSON
He says, still glaring at Levy and desiring to rub it in:

TITLE 154:   "Our beloved cantor is very sick next door—if he
hears you singing, he dies sure."

356. CLOSE SHOT   GROUP
They all start arguing, and Yudelson takes out his watch
and tells the committee that the meeting is over. They
surround him and bombard him with questions as to who
is going to sing. He throws up his hands hopelessly and
starts out of the door, just as the boys of the choir start
arriving.

357.   RABINOWITZ LIVING ROOM
Sara is sitting in the rocking chair, rocking slowly back and
forth. Her eyes are swollen with crying. Her grief has
reached the bottom-most depths. Every few moments she
looks toward the bedroom door as though expecting some
message from the sick chamber.

358.   CLOSE-UP   SARA
As she rocks slowly. She looks toward the bedroom, then
suddenly wipes her eyes and gets up.

359.   FULL SHOT   ROOM
The nurse is just coming out of the door. Sara goes toward
her, but the nurse motions for silence as Sara reaches her
side.

360.   CLOSE-UP   NURSE AND SARA
The nurse whispers to her:

TITLE 155:   "He's asleep."

Sara turns to resume her chair as the nurse goes toward the
kitchen.

361.   EXT. HOUSE
A taxicab drives up quickly, and before it stops Jack is out of
the door. He pays the driver and dashes up the steps. Jack is
dressed for the street in well-tailored but quietly styled
clothes. He rings the bell.

362.   CLOSE-UP   AT DOOR
The door is opened and Sara appears. She looks at Jack in
surprise, then throws her arms around him saying:

TITLE 156:   "You come to sing, Jakie? You come to sing?"

Jack shakes his head saying, "I come to see Papa." They go
into the house.

363. EXT. SYNAGOGUE
The doors are open and there is a steady stream of people entering, Jews, old and young, bearded and clean-shaven, women in shawls and stylish street attire. Occasionally a fine automobile drives up and a prosperous family gets out, while the liveried chauffeur holds open the door. Yom Kippur is about to begin, the one holiday of the year when even the least orthodox Jews think of their religion. It is approaching sundown and the sinking orb is casting long shadows into the East Side street.[19]

364. INT. HOUSE   FULL SHOT   LIVING ROOM
Jack and his mother are standing in the middle of the floor, talking to the nurse. The nurse is shaking her head.

365. CLOSE SHOT   GROUP
The nurse says as she shakes her head that Dr. O'Shaughnessy would not want the sick man's sleep disturbed. Jack pleads with her.

366. CLOSE-UP   JACK
He takes the nurse's arm pleadingly and says:

TITLE 157:   "I'll be awful quiet—I just want to look at him."

367. CLOSE-UP   GROUP
The nurse finally succumbs to Jack's eloquent pleading and starts over toward the bedroom door, followed by Jack and his mother.

368. MED. SHOT   GROUP
They reach the door. The nurse cautions Jack to be very quiet as she slowly opens the door. She motions for Sara to remain behind. Sara bursts into tears as she turns away. Jack enters and the nurse closes the door softly behind him.

369. FULL SHOT   BEDROOM
The old cantor is lying with his eyes closed as Jack enters on

127

tiptoe. He walks very quietly over to the bed where he stands for a moment, then he drops down to his knees beside the bed and gives way to his grief.

370.   CLOSE-UP   JACK AND CANTOR
Jack, with eyes streaming, puts out a hand to touch that of his father, then, fearing that he will wake him with serious results, he withdraws his hand. His shoulders are shaking convulsively with suppressed sobs, and he suddenly buries his face in his hands, which are resting on the bed. The old man's eyelids flutter for a moment. His eyes slowly open and he looks over and sees the bowed head of his son.

371.   CLOSE-UP   CANTOR
There is just the faintest flicker of a smile on the wan face of the dying man. With an effort he slowly moves his hand over until it rests on Jack's head in an unspoken blessing. Jack's hands come up and grasp that of his father.

372.   CLOSE-UP   JACK AND FATHER
With a sudden impulsive gesture Jack grasps the hand of his father and kisses it. Then the old man's eyes close and Jack looks suddenly around to the door.

373.   CLOSE-UP   NURSE AT DOOR
She is motioning for Jack to come out. As she does, the figure of the doctor appears behind her.

374.   FULL SHOT   ROOM
As the doctor enters, Jack goes to the door. He grasps the doctor's hand and the doctor greets him heartily, though quietly. Jack points to the bed in mute inquiry. The doctor says, quietly: "I'm afraid not." He goes toward the bed and Jack with streaming eyes starts slowly out of the room.

375.   EXT. HOUSE
It is now almost dark and lights are beginning to flicker. A taxicab drives up hurriedly and Mary and Lee get out of it.

Lee tells the driver to wait for them. Mary by this time is looking at the number to verify the place. They hurry up the steps and Mary rings the bell.[20]

376. INT. LIVING ROOM   FULL SHOT
Yudelson and Mrs. Rabinowitz are standing at the door of the bedroom as the bell rings. Sara tells Yudelson to go to the door. As he starts for it, the door of the bedroom opens and Jack, wiping his eyes, comes slowly out and into his mother's arms.

377. MED. SHOT   AT DOOR
Yudelson admits Mary and Lee. They both ask at once for Jack, and as they see him they go quickly toward him.

378. CLOSE-UP   JACK AND MOTHER
Jack's attention is attracted by the newcomers. He looks at them in surprise and half pushes his mother away to greet them. He is still in a daze but realizes the nature of their mission.

379. MED. SHOT   GROUP
Mary and Lee each take one of Jack's hands and ply him with questions as to what he is going to do. Yudelson and Sara exchange significant glances.

380. CLOSE-UP   DOOR
Levy the *Shammas* enters hurriedly.

381. FULL SHOT   ROOM
Levy enters and goes quickly to Yudelson. He tells him that the congregation is waiting for the services to begin and suggests that he be designated to sing.

382. CLOSE-UP   TWO MEN
Yudelson greets this suggestion angrily. He yells at Levy:

TITLE 158:   "You don't sing—even if I got to do it myself."

Back. In a crestfallen manner, Levy retires. Yudelson stands and looks at the others speculatively. Then a determined look comes over his features.[21]

383. FULL SHOT ROOM
As Jack argues with Lee and Mary, Sara enters the group. She begs Jack to sing, for the sake of his father. Yudelson walks to the side of the room and takes the cantor's praying shawl and skull cap which are hanging up. He carries them over to Jack and holds them in front of him.

384. CLOSE SHOT GROUP
With Yudelson and his mother on one side and Lee and Mary on the other, Jack is besieged by the old life and the new, filial duty against his life's ambition, the past against the future. He stands staring from one to the other.

385. CLOSE-UP LEE
He holds out his hands appealingly. He says:

TITLE 159: "You can't throw away this one great chance, Jack—the house sold out—and it will ruin me too!"

He looks to Mary for help.

386. CLOSE SHOT GROUP
Mary adds her entreaties to those of Lee, while Sara takes the shawl and cap from Yudelson and holds them out to Jack mutely. Jack looks slowly from Mary to mother, then he stares ahead as though trying to pierce the curtain of the future.

FADE OUT

FADE IN
387. THEATER LOBBY   NIGHT
People in evening clothes are passing into the brilliantly lighted lobby. There is a line at the box office. In the center of the lobby are two large easels containing photographs. Several persons pause before them.

388.　CLOSE-UP　EASELS
One of the easels contains a full-length portrait of Mary Dale in ballet costume and the other a full-length portrait of Jack Robin in blackface. There is a couple standing beside it, and the man says to the woman that this fellow will be the hit of the town. They pass in.

389.　MED. SHOT　LOBBY
The people are still passing into the lobby.
　　　　　　　　　　　　　　　　DISSOLVE INTO:

INT. THEATER[22]
It is a shot from about the center of the audience showing the front part of the house filled with people in evening dress. Several late arrivals enter. The orchestra has presumably just finished the overture when a man in tuxedo steps from behind the curtain at one side of the stage. He walks onto the apron and starts making an announcement.

390.　CLOSE-UP　MAN
He says that he regrets to announce that because of some unforeseen occurrence, the plans for opening the "April Follies" have had to be changed at the last moment, and adds:

TITLE 160:　　"The unfortunate accident to our chief comedian, Mr. Jack Robin, occurred too late to fill his place. We hope that you will pardon . . ."

He continues the announcement, finishes, then bows and makes his exit.

391.　FULL SHOT　THEATER FROM STAGE
The people in the theater are getting up and leaving.
　　　　　　　　　　　　　　　　FADE OUT

FADE IN
392.　FULL SHOT　CANTOR'S BEDROOM
The doctor is at the bedside of the dying man. At the other side sits Sara, while the nurse is busy at a nearby table. Sara

realizes that the end is near, and she is holding the hand of the old man as she weeps quietly.

393. CLOSE-UP BED
The cantor is lying on his back with eyes closed. Just the outline of Sara is visible. (Vitaphone of singing starts very dimly as though from the synagogue next door. As the sound increases in volume, the voice of his son comes into the wailing higher notes of "Kol Nidre.") The old man's eyes open slowly. The misty look slowly clears and, as he recognizes the voice, he looks about him rather wildly. Slowly realization comes to him that his last earthly wish has been granted. With a glorified smile on his face, he mutters: "It's my Jakie." He starts to raise himself slowly. He looks toward the window.

394. FULL SHOT ROOM
As the cantor slowly raises his shattered body, the doctor, anticipating his wish, goes quickly to the window and raises it. (Music of singing becomes much louder.)

395. CLOSE-UP CANTOR
He is raising himself until he is almost sitting up in bed, Sara's arm behind him, helping him. He lifts his eyes to heaven and his lips move in a prayer. Then his eyes close and he falls slowly back to the pillow. The end has come, and Sara throws herself across his body in a paroxysm of grief.

396. FULL SHOT SYNAGOGUE
With the camera in back of place, Jack, with prayer shawl and skullcap on, can be seen with back to congregation. The choir boys are lined up on either side of him, facing the center. His voice is now loud and clear.

397. CLOSE-UP JACK
He is singing, with eyes half closed, one of the wailing passages from the "Kol Nidre."

398. INT. LIVING ROOM   MED. SHOT
     Mary and Lee stand listening. In the background the doctor
     and nurse come quietly out of the bedroom door. The nurse
     goes to the back of the house. The doctor pauses and looks
     at the two listeners, then quietly goes to the front door.

399. CLOSE-UP   MARY AND LEE
     They are still listening as though spellbound. As the vol-
     ume increases, they look from one to the other wonder-
     ingly. Lee says in an awe-stricken voice:

TITLE 161:   "You are listening to the stage's greatest blackface
              comedian singing to his God."

     He looks to Mary for a solution of his problem. Her face
     lights up as Lee shrugs his shoulders in a gesture of resig-
     nation, and she says:

TITLE 162:   "Listen. Don't you understand? It's his last time in
              there. He *has* to come back to us."

     Lee looks at her in a puzzled manner, then nods.

400. INT. SYNAGOGUE   CLOSE-UP   JACK
     He is singing an exceptionally sorrowful passage of the
     "Kol Nidre."

401. MED. SHOT   JACK
     As he comes to the closing notes of the song, the figure of
     the old cantor in his synagogue robes appears on the side of
     the screen very faint and shadowy. The misty form slowly
     comes to the side of the singer. It pauses. There is a smile on
     the face of the old cantor as he slowly raises his hand in a
     blessing. The shadowy figure becomes fainter and fainter,
     finally disappearing, leaving Jack standing alone. The
     music and his figure slowly

                                              FADE OUT[23]

THE END

Annotation to the Screenplay

The preceding screenplay is the original Warner Brothers "Final" of *The Jazz Singer*. It was prepared by Alfred A. Cohn, an all-but-forgotten screenwriter of the silent and early sound eras, during the spring of 1927. (The only date on the script itself is 1927, but studio records indicate that Cohn was assigned to the project on March 14 and that Jolson had read the completed script by mid June.)

According to Cohn's obituary in *Variety* (February 7, 1951), he did his first screenwriting job in 1918 and altogether worked on more than one hundred scripts. His main period of activity was the twenties; *The American Film Institute Catalog, 1921–1930* lists him for twenty-eight titling, writing, or story credits. The most prominent of these, next to *The Jazz Singer*, is *The Cat and the Canary*, which he co-scripted for Universal just before he did *The Jazz Singer*. What probably recommended him most strongly to Warner Brothers was a Jewish-subject specialty in his credit list. He had scripted two of the Irish-Jewish boy-meets-girl romances popular at the time, *The Cohens and Kellys* (1926) and *Frisco Sally Levy* (1927), and he had co-scripted an earlier Lower East Side father-son story, *His People* (1925), which also has a rabbi who throws his son out of the house when he learns the boy has taken up a too-worldly career.

Cohn's script for *The Jazz Singer* is a skillful job of converting the scene structure of a play into the more episodic sequence continuity needed for a film. He also added new opening sequences (scenes 1–138) showing Jakie Rabinowitz's boyhood on the Lower East Side and his early efforts to launch a career as Jack Robin. Brief general instructions for the Vitaphone sequences are also inserted at the appropriate places, but no dialogue is indicated.

Cohn's screenwriting career tapers off in the sound era; his last recorded credit is in 1934. After that he seems to have devoted his principal energies to a career as public servant of the City of Los Angeles, serving, successively, as Collector of Customs, member of the Board of Public Utilities and Transportation, and president of the Police Commission. According to capsule biographies and obituaries, Cohn started as a reporter for a Chicago paper in the 1890s and was also at various times in his career a newspaper editor, magazine editor, columnist, and publicist, as well as

135

the author of several books. Sidney Skolsky's syndicated newspaper column of October 2, 1940, was devoted to Cohn and his reminiscences of "old Hollywood."

Numbers in parentheses refer to scene numbers in the screenplay.

1 Generalized Vitaphone instructions of this sort are inserted throughout the screenplay. See pages 143–46 for details of the synchronized sound sequences.

2 The first part of the film (1–61) is structured differently and is considerably shorter. The organ grinder (4–8), the exterior shots of the synagogue (8–9), and the sequences of the cantor with his class (10–32) and later with Jakie alone (33–36) are all eliminated, and after the opening atmospheric shots of the Lower East Side (see figure 1) the action cuts immediately to the Rabinowitz living room and the conversation between the cantor and his wife about Jakie (44–49). The first "beer garden" sequence (37–43) is moved from before the Rabinowitz conversation to after it, and joined to the second beer garden sequence (50–57), so that the action of Jakie's singing and Yudelson's overhearing and running to tell his parents is played continuously.

3 In the film's intertitles, Yudelson calls them "raggy time songs." Similar changes are made for the same racist characterization in script scenes 77 and 326.

4 An interpolated sequence in the film shows Jakie returning home, weeping over his mother's picture, then leaving for good, while the cantor's singing continues on the soundtrack.

5 George Jessel was replaced by Al Jolson in the role in late May 1927.

6 The material in scenes 96–112 does not appear in the print provided to me. It was apparently shot, however: see Jack L. Warner, *My First Hundred Years in Hollywood* (New York: Random House, 1965), following p. 140, for a photograph of the set.

7 In the film, Buster's role as intermediary is eliminated. After rejoining Buster at their table, Jack receives a congratulatory message from Mary via the headwaiter and goes over to meet her by himself. William Demarest (as Buster Billings) is left with only a very small part in the film.

8 In the film, scenes 138–48 are restructured so that the exchange over Jakie (now Jack) takes place not between the cantor and his young pupil but between the cantor and his wife. In new material added at the end of the sequence, Sara shows the cantor Jack's letter and he explodes, "I told you never to open his letters—*we have no son!*"

9 Scenes 159–61 with Buster Billings do not appear in the film.

10 A sequence not in the script appears at this point in the film. On the road in vaudeville, somewhere in Illinois, August 1927. As the company is waiting for a train, Jack writes Mary a letter telling her he went over big last night and nearly stopped the show. Nearby conversations indicate he is indeed doing well: a buxom and obviously envious middle-aged lady in the company tells a companion that if "that jazz singer" gets her place on the bill again she'll leave the show; she is overheard, and someone says to the others to let her rave, Jack deserves the best spot on the bill. Just as the company is boarding a train, a wire comes from Harry Lee summoning Jack to New York to appear in a Broadway revue. The buxom lady gives her reluctant congratulation, and Jack rushes off to catch the train going in the opposite direction. (There is a small continuity error in the film. Jack's letter to Mary is dated August 7, 1927, but Mary's earlier wire from Harry Lee [see 158] is dated August 8.)

11 Scenes 179–99 do not appear in the film.

12 In the film, as he is leaving, Yudelson bumps into Jack on the doorstep, recognizes him, and the two exchange warm greetings.

13 The main dialogue sequence appears at this point in the film. Jack sings "Blue Skies" to his mother (see figure 8) and interrupts the song to tell her what he's going to do for her if the show is a success.

14 "Hal Bolton" is a thinly disguised allusion to Jolson. Raphaelson had used this name in "The Day of Atonement." The brashness of the suggestion that Jessel might be better than Jolson would be ample cause for making at least a gesture of concealment.

15 The entire subplot in scenes 259–64 and 269–79 involving Dillings's anger over Jack's relationship with Mary, which was in the play, is eliminated in the film. Anders Randolf (as Dillings) only appears briefly in a walk-on, then the film cuts from the rehearsal scenes to the Rabinowitz home, where the cantor lies ill. Yudelson arrives and shows Sara a newspaper headline announcing the opening of the show the following evening (this in place of the insert after 262).

16 A comic sequence with Yudelson at the stage door trying to get in to see Jack appears here in the film. (Some of the material from scenes 271–87 is incorporated into it.) When the doorkeeper points to a No Admittance sign, Yudelson shrugs, "Who's smoking?" Yudelson asks for Jakie Rabinowitz, "the ector," and he is in obvious discomfort when he is left to wait beside an ample showgirl in shorts (see figure 11).

17 Scenes 296–98, 303–5, and 310–11 with Yudelson and Mrs. Rubin do not appear in the film. Rather, the scenes of Yudelson and the trust-

ees contemplating the problem that there is no one to sing for the Day of Atonement (350–56) are moved forward and inserted in their place.

18 At scene 323 in the film is another extended sequence at the stage door before the visitors are announced. This time Sara pleads with the doorkeeper to be let in because Jack's father is gravely ill.

19 The exterior shots in scenes 361 and 363 do not appear in the film.

20 This scene does not appear in the film. A substantial addition is made at the beginning of this sequence. Yudelson arrives before Harry Lee and Mary, is surprised to see Jack, tells him the choir is waiting, and pleads with him to come and sing. Sara adds the entreaty that if Jack sings perhaps the cantor will get well.

21 Scenes 380–82 do not appear in the film.

22 This scene is unnumbered in the screenplay.

23 The film adds an epilogue in which Jack appears to a packed house at the Winter Garden theater and sings "Mammy" in blackface (see figure 18) as Sara and Yudelson beam radiantly in the audience.

Production Credits

Director	Alan Crosland
Scenario	Alfred A. Cohn
Source	The story, "The Day of Atonement" (1922), by Samson Raphaelson, and its stage adaptation, *The Jazz Singer* (1925), by Raphaelson, produced by Al Lewis and Max Gordon in association with Sam H. Harris
Photography	Hal Mohr
Editor	Harold McCord
Titles	Jack Jarmuth
Technicians	Fred Jackman, Lewis Geib, Esdras Hartley, F. N. Murphy, "Alpharetta," Victor Vance
Orchestral Score and Direction	Louis Silvers
Sound	George R. Groves
Assistant Director	Gordon Hollingshead

The Jazz Singer was shot during June, July, and August of 1927. Principal photography was at the Warner Brothers studios on Sunset Boulevard in Hollywood. (Exterior scenes of New York were shot on location on the Lower East Side and in front of the Shuberts' Winter Garden theater at Broadway and Forty-ninth Street by Alan Crosland.) Exterior scenes not involving the main performers were shot in California in June. The New York scenes were then shot the latter part of June. Work on the main Jolson silent sequences began in Hollywood in July. Jolson's complicated Vitaphone sequences were done mainly in the latter part of August.

The production was under the direct supervision and control of Sam Warner, who had moved in from the East to take personal charge of this landmark production in the studio's history, and his brother Jack. (According to the program, credit for "the faithful portrayal of Jewish home life" in the film is largely due to yet another Warner, Benjamin, father of the producers and an "ardent admirer of *The Jazz Singer*.")

Jolson sang five popular songs (or excerpts) for the film—"Dirty Hands, Dirty Face," "Toot, Toot, Tootsie," "Blue Skies," "Mother of Mine, I Still Have You," and "My Mammy." He also sang excerpts in Aramaic from the liturgical prayer "Kol Nidre." Composer-pianist Paul Lamkoff, a cantor himself, coached Jolson for his "Kol Nidre" sequence and also supervised the choral backgrounds (*Down Beat*, December 17, 1952, p. 22; Lamkoff was employed in the same capacity with Danny Thomas for the 1952 remake). Bobby (or Bobbie) Gordon apparently sang his own numbers—choruses of "My Gal Sal" and "Waiting for the Robert E. Lee." Famed Cantor Josef Rosenblatt made a personal appearance singing the "Yahrzeit," a secular eulogy for the dead. Hungarian tenor Joseph Diskay dubbed Warner Oland's voice for his "Kol Nidre" sequence (*Variety*, September 7, 1927, p. 11). The synchronized musical score, played by the Vitaphone Orchestra, consisted of excerpts from classical works, orchestral versions of some of the Jolson selections, and orchestrations of popular songs (see "Musical Score," pages 182–83).

The Jazz Singer was also released in a silent version for theaters not yet equipped for Vitaphone.

When the film was remade in 1952, the following information appeared in the *New York Times*: "The making of this new *Jazz Singer* is fraught with nostalgic memories not only for the three remaining Warner brothers but for several of their employees. The picture's property master, 'Limey' Plews, and electrician Ralph Owen worked on the original venture; Harold McCord, now head of the film editing department, cut the first *Jazz Singer* and Alan Crosland Jr., whose father directed that distant screen epic, now is serving as film editor for Mr. Curtiz" (August 10, 1952, II:3).

According to Philip French in *The Movie Moguls* (Chicago: Regnery, 1969), Hal B. Wallis worked on the publicity for *The Jazz Singer* (p. 153).

The Jazz Singer opened at the Warners theater on Broadway near Fifty-second Street in New York on October 6, 1927.

Cast

Jakie Rabinowitz, later	
Jack Robin	Al Jolson
Mary Dale	May McAvoy
Cantor Rabinowitz	Warner Oland
Sara Rabinowitz	Eugenie Besserer
Moisha Yudelson	Otto Lederer
Jakie, age thirteen	Bobby Gordon
Harry Lee	Richard Tucker
Himself, in Concert Number	Cantor Josef Rosenblatt
Levi	Nat Carr
Buster Billings	William Demarest
Dillings	Anders Randolf
Doctor	Will Walling
Agent	Roscoe Karns
Chorus Girls	Myrna Loy, Audrey Ferris
Extras in Coffee Dan's	
Sequence	Jane Arden, Violet Bird, Ernest Clauson, Marie Stapleton, Edna Gregory, Margaret Oliver

Appendix 1

The Synchronized Sound Sequences

The sound track of *The Jazz Singer* was originally recorded on sixteen-inch Vitaphone discs with a playing time of approximately nine minutes each. (In the 1930s these were transferred to optical sound tracks.) Eight sequences in the film contained musical performances with lyrics; two of these, the third and the fifth, also contained synchronized speech. Synchronized sound effects were also occasionally used, as when the trains depart and arrive at the station where Jack gets the call to come to New York, and when Yudelson raps on the table to bring the trustees of the synagogue to order after they learn the cantor will not be able to sing for Yom Kippur, the Day of Atonement.

Descriptions of the eight sound sequences and transcriptions of the dialogue follow:

1. *Young Jakie Rabinowitz Sings* (see figure 3)

A piano player in a neighborhood beer garden introduces thirteen-year-old "Ragtime Jakie," who sings a chorus of "My Gal Sal." Yudelson hears him from the adjoining barroom and hurries off to the Rabinowitz home to tell the cantor he has just seen his son singing ragtime songs in a saloon. As the cantor sets off to investigate, we cut back to Jakie going into a new number, "Waiting for the Robert E. Lee." From the doorway the cantor sees his son on stage singing and "shufflin'." He rushes in and Jakie stops his song in mid line.

2. *Cantor Rabinowitz Sings "Kol Nidre"* (see figure 4)

After getting a whipping, Jakie runs away, and the cantor goes to eve of the Day of Atonement services alone. For music and bilingual texts of "Kol Nidre," see Abraham Idelson, ed., and Baruch Joseph Cohon, mus. ed., *The Jewish Song Book for Synagogue, School and Home*, 3d ed., rev. and enl. (Cincinnati: Publications for Judaism, 1951), pp. 248–59.

143

Appendix 1

3. *Jack Robin Appears at Coffee Dan's* (see figure 5)

Years later Jakie Rabinowitz, now Jack Robin, an unknown jazz singer, gets a chance to appear at Coffee Dan's, a popular San Francisco nightspot and showcase for amateur performers. He sings a song (written by Jolson and two others) about the joys of having an endearing young son, "Dirty Hands, Dirty Face."

It is received with enthusiastic applause. Jack raises his hand to stop it and addresses the audience: "Wait a minute! Wait a minute! You ain't hear nothin' yet. Wait a minute, I tell ya, you ain't heard nothin'! You wanna hear 'Toot, Toot, Tootsie!'? All right, hold on, hold on. Lou, listen: Play 'Toot, Toot, Tootsie!' Three choruses, you understand. In the third chorus I whistle. Now give it to 'em hard and heavy. Go right ahead."*

He sings it through once, whistles the chorus, then shouts to the band, as the next chorus begins, "Get hot!" In singing it again, he varies the words (for example, from "Tootsie" to "Tootie," from "hey, hey" to "dah, dah"); it was said of Jolson that he never sang a song the same way twice.

4. *Cantor Rosenblatt Sings*

In Chicago Jack Robin attends a matinee concert of religious music performed by famed Cantor Josef Rosenblatt. Cantor Rosenblatt sings the "Yahrzeit," a secular eulogy sung on the anniversary of a death preceding the recital of the *Kaddish*.

5. *Jack Robin Comes Home and Sings for Mother* (see figure 8)

Jack gets a chance to appear in a Broadway revue and he returns to New York. The day of his homecoming is the cantor's sixtieth birthday. After an emotional reunion with his mother, he tells her about his big break and sings and plays for her Irving Berlin's "Blue Skies," the song he's going to do in the show.

After one chorus, Jack turns from the piano and speaks to his mother. Throughout this exchange her replies and protestations are heard very faintly and indistinctly:

JACK: Did you like that, Mama?
MOTHER: Yes.

*The "Lou" Jack calls to is Lou Silvers, musical director of the film, who plays the piano in the band.

JACK: I'm glad of it. I'd rather please you than anybody I know of. Oh, darlin', will you give me something?

MOTHER: What?

JACK: You'll never guess. Shut your eyes, Mama. Shut 'em for little Jakie. Ha. I'm gonna steal something. (Kisses her. She titters.) Ha, ha, ha, ha. I'll give it back to you some day, too, you see if I don't. Mama, darlin', if I'm a success in this show, well, we're gonna move from here. Oh yes, we're gonna move up in the Bronx. A lot of nice green grass up there and a whole lot of people you know. There's the Ginsbergs, the Guttenbergs, and the Goldbergs. Oh, a whole lotta Bergs; I don't know 'em all. And I'm gonna buy you a nice black silk dress, Mama. You see Mrs. Friedman, the butcher's wife, she'll be jealous of you.

MOTHER: Oh no—

JACK: Yes, she will. You see if she isn't. And I'm gonna get you a nice pink dress that'll go with your brown eyes.

MOTHER: No, Jakie, no I–I–I–

JACK: What? Whatta you mean, no? Who is—who is telling you? Whatta you mean, no? Yes, you'll wear pink or else. Or else you'll wear pink. (He laughs.) And, darlin', oh, I'm gonna take you to Coney Island.

MOTHER: Yeah?

JACK: Yes, I'm gonna ride on the Shoot-the-Chutes. An' you know in the Dark Mill? Ever been in the Dark Mill?

MOTHER: Oh, no. I wouldn't go . . .

JACK: Well, with me, it's all right. I'll kiss you and hug you. You see if I don't. (Mother starts blushing.) Now Mama, Mama, stop now. You're gettin' kittenish. Mama, listen, I'm gonna sing this like I will if I go on the stage. You know, with this show. I'm gonna sing it jazzy. Now get this . . .

and he launches into a few more lines of the song. He bangs at the keyboard with his right hand and turns to Mama and asks, "Do you like that slappin' business?" As he is singing the next part, the cantor enters in the background and cries out "Stop!"

6. *Jack Robin Sings in Dress Rehearsal* (see page 10)

With the cantor ill, Sara Rabinowitz and Yudelson visit Jack at the theater and plead with him to come and sing for Day of Atonement services. It is opening day of the show, "April Follies," and Jack goes on for dress rehearsal in blackface and sings "Mother of Mine, I Still Have You." Written by Jolson and Lou Silvers, it reflects the story by addressing a brokenhearted mother whose wandering son returns to her arms from the less constant outside world.

7. *Jack Robin Sings at Day of Atonement Services* (see figure 17)

Jack leaves the theater and goes to see his dying father. The opening performance of "April Follies" is canceled. Jack sings "Kol Nidre" in his father's place.

8. *Jack Robin Sings "Mammy"*(see figure 18)

"The season passes—and time heals—the show goes on." At the Winter Garden theater, with Sara and Yudelson in the audience and Mary looking on from the wings, Jack sings "My Mammy."

Appendix 2

The Day of Atonement

*So Sound and Dramatic Is this Tale That a Manager Plans
to Make a Play of It. The Author Confesses That He Isn't
the Idol of Millions of Readers Now, but We Predict That He
Will Make Friends Fast*

By Sampson Raphaelson

"What Jack Robin needs," said David Lee, who owns some of the whitest of Broadway's white lights, "is a wife."

"What our Jakie needs," said Jack Robin's father, old Cantor Rabinowitz, of the Hester Street Synagogue, "is a God."

"What I need," said Jack Robin, "is a song-number with a kick in it. The junk that Tin Pan Alley is peddling these days is rusty—that's all—*rusty*."

And the sum and substance of it was a sober-faced Jack, engaged fitfully in experiments with pleasure, a worried but watchful David Lee, and a tragically lonely household on Hester Street, where dwelt the aged cantor and his wife.

For Jack was no ordinary singer of ragtime. Those dark eyes of his might have been the ecstatic eyes of a poet in the days when the Chosen People lived sedately in the land of Canaan. They might have been prophetic eyes, stern and stirring, in the years of Zedekiah, son of Josiah, King of Judah, when Jerusalem "knew not its God." They might have been deep wells of lamentation even one generation ago had his lyric voice been born to cry the sorrows of Israel in a Russian synagogue.

But he lived in New York, and his slender, well-set-up figure was draped in perfectly fitting suits of Anglo-Saxon severity, and his dark hair was crisply trimmed and parted after the fashion of young America, and the black eyes in his thin, handsome face were restless, cynical and without joy.

Everybody's Magazine, January 1922, pp. 44–55. © 1921, renewed 1949, Sampson Raphaelson. Reprinted by permission. Raphaelson changed the spelling of his given name from Sampson to Samson when *The Jazz Singer* was produced.

That bewilderment, brooding and fitful, which was now so palpable, had vaguely begun to propel Jack in the days when, as Jakie Rabinowitz, he had drifted with a gang of Hester Street hoodlums. He was twelve then, rather tall and sturdy for his age, and for an exciting few weeks he enjoyed the thrills of looting fruit-stands, of stealing milk-bottles and of openly shooting craps. But the bliss of these few weeks came to a hysterical termination when he violated the code of the gang, and it was not until ten years later, when he knew Amy Prentiss, that he felt such happiness again.

The gang's code regarded certain acts of loyalty as religion, and certain epithets could be avenged only in blood—the blood of a bleeding nose or a lacerated lip. Foremost among the firebrand epithets was the term "sheeny." If some one called you a sheeny, only one thing could properly ensue—violent fistic battle. But Jakie, traversing Cherry Street, the Irish domain, received the stigma with indifference.

He and nine-year-old Hymie Cohen were on their way home from an East River salt-water swimming-shack, where for a dime they had received the use of faded trunks and the privileges of a moldy wooden tank. A barefoot young "mick," slighter than Jakie but of truculent demeanor, had united ten fingers with his nose in a trestle of vilification and cried: "Yah! Lookit the sheeny! Go back where yah came from, yah sheeny!"

Jakie shrugged his shoulders and passed on. Neither righteous indignation nor the tremors of fear had risen within him.

Little Hymie told his big brother Joe of the humiliating incident, and that night Joe asked Jakie about it.

"Yah didn't fight, did yah?" he demanded. "Yah didn't do nothin'?"

"Why should I fight? I wasn't mad."

Joe stepped close to Jakie.

"You're yeller! Yah got a yeller streak a mile wide right t'rough to your liver! Yah can't hang around wit' de gang no more. Go 'way before I paste yah one on the jaw!"

This was disturbing. Jakie was not minded to obedient alacrity. He responded with a show of spirit,

"I'll go when I feel like it!"

Joe's response was a contemptuous slap over the eyes—a slap which stung and infuriated. Sobbing and seeing red, Jakie fell upon Joe and blindly pommeled away with his fists.

After it was over and Jakie lay on the curb with a "shiner," a bleeding nose, and a perforated dental display, sobbing breathlessly and cursing in richly filthy East Side *argot*, Joe came up to him.

" I take it back, Jakie," he said, proffering his hand. "Y'ain't yeller. I—"

"Go to hell," Jakie panted, "you dirty sheeny!"

Jakie went directly home that night and endured stoically his father's scolding and his mother's running fire of questions. Dwelling in a passion of hatred for the complete order of things, his parents exasperated him into a seething calm beyond the point of articulate resentment. The next day he played truant from Hebrew school.

The *Melammed*, who was receiving a dollar a month extra for teaching the cantor's son, anxious to prepare him magnificently for the *Bar Mitzvah* recitative and speech in the synagogue, went out in search of the boy. He found Jakie playing basket-ball in the Hester Street playgrounds, dragged him back to the small, ill-smelling, gas-lit room where a few of the older boys still were singsonging the cadenced subtleties of *"Baba Kama,"* and flogged him until his body was purple.

Jakie came home that night somewhat terrified by the decision he had made, yet completely set in his determination. He was acute enough to speak to his mother first.

"Mamma, that *Rebi*—he ain't no good. He's so *dirty*, and he's always hollering, and, anyways, none of us kids ever learns anything. And he nearly killed me to-day, mamma, with a big strap— Look how sore my back is—and I never did nothing at all!"

"I'll tell papa," said his mother, busily applying goose-grease to his tortured back, "and he'll speak to the *Rebi* he shouldn't hit you no more."

"I don't wanna go to *Chaidar*," Jakie announced, with low-voiced intensity.

"Jakie! Your papa shouldn't hear you speak like this! How could you ever be a *Chazon*—a cantor in a big fancy synagogue—if you don't know good your Hebrew? I'll speak to papa he should find you a new *Chaidar* and a new *Rebi*."

"I don't want no new *Chaidar*, and I don't want to be a *Chazon* when I grow up!"

"Jakie! Eat your supper and don't speak it another word like this! Lucky your papa he's ain't home, or he would kill you."

The boy did not move toward the table. He raised a blazing face to his mother.

"If papa kills me," he said, "then I'll run away from home."

The old cantor did whip Jakie. It had long been a matter of profound distress to the cantor that a youth with so nimble a mind should be so diffident in the presence of the great culture of the noblest of all peoples. For ten generations, in Russia and now in America, the name "Rabinowitz" had stood for devout, impassioned *Chazonoth*, and Jakie's father was animated by the one desire that his son should become even a greater cantor than himself.

"I can see it comes a day when the Children of Israel will need it more *Chazonim*," the old father had said once to his young son. "It's too good here in America—too much money—too much telephones and trains and ragtime. A little bit more God ain't a bad thing, Jakie. Music is God's voice, and you make it your papa and mamma happy, Jakie, if you grow up to be a great *Chazon* like your grandfather in Vilna *olav-hasholom*."

"Aw, gee," Jakie had responded; "I wish the *Rebi* would comb his whiskers onct in a while!"

Fervently considering his God, the cantor had beaten Jakie soberly, and the boy had been inclined after that to listen in silence, if with resentment, to his pleas and homilies. That beating a year ago was the first Jakie had suffered from his father. The present belaboring was the second and last. That night, while his parents slept, Jakie, true to his word, did run away from home.

A policeman found him, two days later, white with hunger and dragging his feet with weariness. His parents, who had become panic-stricken, overfed him and put him tenderly to bed. In the next few days they argued and pleaded with him, and, before they admitted defeat, wept before him.

"I'll sing in the choir every Sabbath," he said then. "But, honest, pa, *honest*, I'd quicker die than go every day to a *Chaidar*."

His father had to find comfort during the several years that followed in hearing the liquid golden tones of Jakie's alto voice in the choir only on Sabbath and on holy days.

"Maybe," he said to his wife, "maybe when he gets older, he'll see how beautiful is *Yiddishkeit*. Maybe he would stop hanging around music-places and singing these ragtime songs what all the bums they sing."

"I'm afraid, Yosele; I'm afraid," she sighed. "When he grows older, a job he'll get it—in a tailor shop, maybe—and right away with a girl he'll be running around."

"Better he should never marry," the cantor cried, "than with one of these peek-a-boo-waist girls with paint on the faces! Oy, Rivka mine, why ain't it here in America good healthy girls like you was?"

But girls were not in Jakie's mind. The few who moved through his life had laughed too much and listened too little. They were shrill creatures, made for anything but love. They were haughty when they should have been humbly eager, and they greedily mimicked things they should austerely have left alone.

He might have sunk to a Russian kind of morbidness if he had not been caught up in the stream of highly seasoned folk-song which poured constantly from Tin Pan Alley.

By the time he was eighteen he moved in an unreal, syncopated world of his own. If he had a sentimental grief, what better relief than sitting in the dark of his bedroom in the tiny Hester Street flat and howling dolefully the strains of "Down by the Old Mill Stream"? If the joys of being alive smote him, what could more sweetly ease the ache of happiness than the plaintive blare of "Alexander's Ragtime Band"?

So he haunted the motion-picture shows.

Then one night he got a job singing popular songs in the Great Alcazar Palace on Grand Street—one of the new movie-houses with rococo modeling in front, a house penetrating into the bowels of the building to a greater depth than its rickety, makeshift predecessors. And later that night his father told him never to show his face in the Hester Street home again.

"Better I shouldn't have it no son at all. Your loafer's talk stabs me in my heart. I couldn't bear to see your face no more—bum! In a synagogue you don't even put your head. For ten generations was every Rabinowitz a God-fearing *Chazon*, and you—my only son—street-songs you are singing! Go! Be a ragtime singer with the bums!"

How could the old cantor, or, for that matter, Jakie himself, understand that instead of being sinful and self-indulgent, loose and lazy, this grave-eyed boy with the ways of the street was sincerely carrying on the tradition of plaintive, religious melody of his forefathers—carrying on that tragic tradition disguised ironically with the gay trappings of Broadway and the rich vulgarity of the East Side? Instinctively the East Side responded to it, for people came hours early to the Great Alcazar Palace and stood in line twenty deep to hear Jakie, now Jack Robin, sing "Lovey Joe" or "When Dat Midnight Choo-Choo Leaves for Alabam'."

"Chee, but that baby can rag!" they said, as they swayed, hypnotized, to the caressing quavers of his voice. They knew only that he caught at their heart-strings. They failed to perceive that Jakie was simply translating the age-old music of the cantors—that vast loneliness of a race wandering "between two worlds, one dead, the other powerless to be born"—into primitive and passionate Americanese.

One year Jakie spent thus, and then David Lee, on a periodical scouting expedition, drifted into the Great Alcazar Palace. A short, fat man with cold blue eyes in a round pink face, Lee slipped unnoticed into the dark of the last row. He heard Jack Robin render "Underneath the Sugar Moon" with swifter, more potent tunefulness than a certain black-face comedian whom he was paying a thousand a week for singing the same song on Broadway. As a result, Jack Robin found himself booked on the great Keats vaudeville circuit.

"It's up to you," David Lee told him. "If you can put it over in vaudeville for a year or two, I'll place you on Broadway in electric lights."

With money and comfort and prestige tossed into his lap, a certain change came slowly over Jack. The clouds, lifting away, did not reveal sunshine, but a gray void. The clouds had been grim, inexplicable, tormenting—but they had inspired. The present void was reflected by emptiness in Jack. He was singing badly when he encountered Amy Prentiss, who was billed by the Keats people as "The World-Famous Dancer of Joyous Dances."

It was in San Francisco. Her act preceded his, and he stood in the wings, waiting his turn. Slender, dark-haired, blue-eyed, she had none of the Oriental instinct for undulation which Jack had understood so easily and to which he was so casually indifferent. Her open, frankly gay movements, her girlishly graceful fluttering pricked him to a breathless interest. She was bafflingly foreign to him—everything about her. Elusive, infinitely desirable to his naturally complex nature because of her simplicity, *she* was seeing the sunshine which for him did not exist. As he stood there watching, Henrietta Mooney, of the Mooney Ballet, joined him.

Henrietta's name off-stage was Sadie Rudnick. Jack had seen her performance several times in the past few years, and, while it was skilful and had its charm, its qualities were no mystery to him. Nor was Henrietta herself a mystery, for with one glance Jack knew her as baldly as he would a sister. "A clever Grand Street kid—in her second youth."

Henrietta listened in the wings at this Monday matinée while Jack went through his performance. She was there when he came off, and came directly up to him, saying without preliminaries,

"Kiddo, I heard you last September in Chicago, and you're losing the wallop."

Jack smiled without replying.

"What's wrong?" the girl persisted. "Booze?"

Jack shook his head amiably.

"Is it a skirt?"

"No; and it isn't an off day, either," he said wearily. "Guess I'm just getting tired of the game."

"Bunk!" was her scornful response. "You were born to the profession."

With the easy fellowship of the stage, they became chummy during the week. They would stand idly in the wings during the greater part of the performances, exchanging comments and gossip. Jack liked Henrietta's sturdy honesty, her slangy sophistication. Saturday evening, as he was hungrily following the fairylike movements of Amy Prentiss, Henrietta said,

"That girl's got your goat!"

"Do you think so?"

"Say—do I *think* so? I *know* it!"

"I wonder why," he mused audibly.

Henrietta looked him squarely in the eyes.

"You wonder why? She's a *Shiksa*; that's why! I've seen Jewish boys fall that way before. It ain't new to me." There was bitterness in her voice.

"But why?" Jack repeated, more to himself than to her. "Why?"

"You come from the Ghetto, and she studied fancy dancing in a private school. You're the son of a poor old *Chazon*, and she's the daughter of a Boston lawyer. You're— Aw, you make me sick!"

Abruptly Henrietta left him, and during the one remaining day of their stay in San Francisco she avoided him. But her words stayed with him; they pried brutally into his apathy; they jeered him from afar; they came terribly close and stung him. The thought of approaching this lovely dancer with the quiet eyes and the gentle mouth frightened him a little; but his fear angered him. As she came out into the wings Saturday night, she found him in her path.

"Say—" he began. She stopped, smiling uncertainly. Jack, to her, was a pleasingly debonair figure with a handsome face, glowing eyes. His manner she hadn't the time or the gift to analyze.

"I have to hand it to you," he went on, self-consciously, flushing to the roots of his hair. "You—you dance with more real class—I mean to say—you're darn good—" He paused, floundering.

It is a curious fact that often the only signs of yearning, of sincere and painful humbleness, of profound anxiety to express fine things consist of awkwardness—of a stilted nonchalance. His confusion served simply to embarrass her. She strove, not in vain, for poise to cover her embarrassment. Her only recourse was to smile vaguely and say, "Glad you liked—uh—" And then, fearing that he might gurgle more badly still, she passed on.

Jack hated her for having made it so hard for him.

"I know she don't care a damn about me," he told himself savagely. "But she didn't have to make a fool of me. She could have said a few civil words, even if I don't mean anything in her life."

In San Diego, in Dallas, in San Antonio, in New Orleans and in the other cities he made on the long swing back to New York, his eyes seemed

153

to seek morbidly for further evidences of the simple, unruffled Anglo-Saxon quality of temperament. He found plenty of them, and, as the weeks passed, they served to beat him down into a soothing numbness, which was bad for the audiences, who sat stonily through his performances. Henrietta's words would constantly drum into his ears: "You come from the Ghetto, and she's the daughter of a Boston lawyer."

It was slowly, because he was fundamentally temperate, that he learned to seek self-respect in barrooms. No one else would have called it that. It had too little of the nature of peace. It brought back the invigorating uncertainty, the inspiring restlessness of his adolescent days. It eliminated, for the moment, this new numbness which had come upon him, this queer sensation of being softly strangled. And, since it substituted his old *Weltschmerz* for the feeling of being slowly buried into a grave of inarticulateness by the Amy Prentisses of the world, his ragtime singing got back some of its old lilting plaintiveness.

Jack saw his parents occasionally. His mother's furtive pride in the adulation which younger Hester Street gave to her son had even begun to reflect itself in a way in the old cantor.

"Every actor he's ain't a loafer, Yosele," she would say. "Look—is Jacob Adler a loafer? A finer man you couldn't find it if you should search a whole lifetime."

"But he's a *Yiddisher* actor, *Leben*. He feels the *Yiddishe* heart. And our Jakie sings ragtime—like a *Shagetz!*"

"I know—I know," she soothed him. "But he's an American boy. And he's a good boy. He's sending you and me presents only last month from New Haven. He lives a clean life, Yosele. Maybe soon he makes enough money and he goes into business and gets married and comes regular every Sabbath and holy day to the synagogue."

When he visited them in the summer, Jack's dumb unhappiness became apparent to them. They took it for a good sign—for indication of a new, more mature thoughtfulness. His booking for the year ended, he took a month's vacation and spent two weeks of it in New York. For two consecutive Sabbath days he attended the synagogue, and the old cantor, singing from the pulpit, exulted in the conviction that his son was returning to his God.

Indeed, Jack himself found a certain solace in it. As he sat on the old familiar wooden bench, clothed in the silk *Talis*—the prayer-shawl which his father had so solemnly presented to him on the occasion of his *Bar Mitzvah*—with good old Yudelson, the cobbler, on one side of him, and stout, hearty, red-bearded Lapinsky, the butcher, on the other, he felt a singular warmth and sweetness. And the voice of his father, still clear and lyric, rising in the intricacies of the familiar old lamenting prayers—prayers which he remembered perfectly, which he would never forget—the dissonant rumble of response from the congregation, the restive shufflings of youngsters—all these were to him blessedly familiar and blissful.

In the murmurous peacefulness of those two weeks his father talked to him constantly of the austere beauties of the ancient ways of his people, and it began to appear to Jack that there was indeed something to be said for them. He could not and did not dismiss his father's world as he used to—with a sneer and the words: "Dead! I tell you that stuff's behind the times." For he began to feel that if it was a dead or a dying world, still it possessed some reality, an orderly nobility; while the world he was alive to was chaotic, crassly unreal.

During the two weeks which followed in Atlantic City he thought a good deal on this, but the nearness of violins and cocktails, the flash of women and the glamour of moonlight on the sea made it easy for him to decide arbitrarily that it was rather an abstract problem.

In Buffalo, where he opened with his act, he began committing the unforgivable sin in the theatrical world—he began missing performances. He had lost all vital interest in his work.

By the time he was playing in Chicago, reports of his derelictions had reached David Lee, who, after long pondering, wrote a severe note.

"What Jack Robin needs," Lee said to Harry Anthony, his partner, "is a wife." In his note he said:

> If I can't depend on a performer being steadily on the job, no matter if he has the genius of Booth and the popularity of George Cohan, I will not have him in my employ. I don't know what's ailing you, but whatever it is, you must steady down. There isn't a producer or booking-office in New York that will gamble on you if you're not completely dependable, and we're no exception.

Jack smiled crookedly when he read this. It came at a most unfortunate time, for, having arrived in Chicago that morning, Jack had discovered that the sixth number on the bill with him at the Majestic was "The World-Famous Dancer of Joyous Dances."

And this discovery was sending him sauntering, blithely bitter, to Righeimer's bar.

It was two in the afternoon. His act went on at three. The act of the girl whose unseen nearness possessed the power to slash him into bewilderment would begin at four. If he left the theatre promptly after his act, most

155

likely he could avoid seeing her. And, with a comforting cargo of Righeimer's product on board, he felt he would be able to give an account of himself on the stage.

To make doubly sure that the sense of Amy's nearness would not cause his heart to sink before the footlights, he took three or four extra drinks. They more than achieved their purpose. The world became an insignificant turmoil underneath his feet, and he strolled, his smile growing steadily more crooked, down Clark Street toward Madison, where at the Morrison bar they could mix the finest Tom Collins in the world. The words of David Lee's letter came into his mind. " 'Completely dependable'—that's me! I'll drink all the Tom Collinses Jerry can mix—to the great god Dependability."

He halted in the crush of traffic on the corner, and, not two feet away from him, jammed by a fat woman on one side and grabbed at on the other by two sticky children, he saw Amy Prentiss. As his eyes glimpsed her proud little head, brown-toqued, quaintly half veiled, his lips compressed into a straight line and he turned sharply away. But the crowd began to move; Amy had seen him, and she was already edging her way toward him. Her face smiled a friendly greeting, and involuntarily Jack looked behind him to see if it were not some one else she was addressing.

"Why, Mr. Robin!" she was saying. "I was just going to the house early to see your turn."

Jack was dumb. They crossed Madison Street together in the surge of the released crowd.

"How did you happen to recognize me?" he blurted.

"You recognized *me*, didn't you?"

"Oh, I recognized you, all right." Jack paused. He longed for an hour in solitude, so that he could think. "This gets me," he confessed. "Your knowing me so quickly, and your actually going early to see my act."

"You're funny. Hasn't anybody let you in on the secret that you're one of the few real rag-singers in America? As for remembering you, how could I ever forget your genuine little compliment on my act out on the Coast?"

They had turned the corner at Monroe Street and were at the entrance to the Majestic. Jack looked hurriedly at his watch.

"Listen," he said; "I have to speed like the deuce to make it. I want to see you—talk to you some more. Meet me after your turn."

His mind raced in zigzags as he hastened to his dressing-room. He searched his memory for the exact wording of Amy's remark that Saturday in San Francisco, for her expression. He tried to see and hear again the outward things and to give a new, inner meaning to them. But all he could recall was the bitterness in him, the significant and fateful words of Henrietta, and Amy's vagueness, which turned the knife in his wounded vanity. And now she had voluntarily talked to him; she was deliberately coming to see him perform; she had been pleasant, approachable, inviting. His mind could find no place for such a manifestation from this girl.

His performance that matinée was discouragingly poor. Amy made no comment on it when they met.

"Let's have dinner somewhere," Jack suggested. "That is"—a flicker of his old wretchedness returning—"that is, if you haven't made any other arrangements, and—and if—"

"I should be glad to."

They dined at the Café Lafayette, which has a sedate lower floor and an upper floor with an orchestra for dancing. It had been in Jack's mind to avoid the beat of syncopated music, but by the time they reached the restaurant, the sweet poise of the girl had filled him with unreasoning dismay at himself. The old familiar bewildered sinking of the heart followed. And so he led her up-stairs. A violin was weaving a slim pattern of simple melody, which was being tortured into savage bedlam by the bulletlike spitting of the drum and by the saxophone's gusts of passionate whining.

He felt instinctively that liquor was not on the cards. But he was tense, strung up, dreadfully nervous.

"Let's dance," he said.

The music was sending forth a one-step, and Jack gave himself to it hungrily. He seemed, somehow, to make of the simple steps a wild, heart-breaking aria, a mad pounding on the doors of heaven.

Back at the table they sat a while in silence. Amy studied his face. She said,

"You dance differently from any one I know."

Jack flushed.

"I don't suppose I dance very well. I—I wish I could dance standing straight and moving sort of—well, evenly and correctly, if you know what I mean. Like that fellow, for instance." He indicated a tall, stolid-looking youth who was soberly and skilfully maneuvering a sleek young creature about the polished floor.

"That's funny," Amy remarked. "I'm crazy about the way you dance. I never quite liked any one's dancing so well. You danced to-night the way you used to sing—the way you sang when I first heard you in New York."

"You *like* my dancing?" Jack leaned to her, unbelieving. His voice came huskily. "*You* don't dance that way—even on the stage. You dance more like that fellow. I don't mean stiff as him—not that. But you're his kind, if you know what I mean. I'm—I'm crazy about that quality in you. I'd give anything if I could have it—that careless, happy— Guess I'm talking like a fool," he ended lamely.

But Amy, her eyes aglow, was leaning to him.

"You're the *funniest* person! I've been crazy about the very thing in you that you're deprecating. I wish I had it. I'd give *anything* to have it. It—it hurt me a lot to find your performance to-day lacking in it."

They dined and danced together every day that week. There was no making of appointments after that evening; tacitly they met after Amy's turn and went out together. Jack went about in an unreal world. He tried to think, but his mind persisted in substituting the turn of Amy's wrist, the curve of her cheek, the gay animation of her eyes, the little liquid turns in her voice.

Each day he grew more afraid of her while she was with him and more desolate while she was not. His only interludes were when they danced. The blare of the orchestra had somehow for him become Music—a glorious substitute for tears, a gleaming speedway for a breathless race hand in hand with grief. Sunday evening—the last of the week they would have together—he found himself holding Amy crushingly close, and he relaxed sharply, dancing badly after that.

Back at the table, sitting side by side on an upholstered bench against the wall, Amy chattered happily until she became aware that Jack was not listening. His food untouched, he was staring with undisguised misery before him. Amy placed her hand lightly over his on the seat.

"What is it?" she asked.

He withdrew his hand, afraid. For a moment he was silent, and Amy repeated her question.

"I—I suppose you think I'm out of my head, but—I—I'm crazy about you."

"I'm crazy about you, too," said Amy promptly.

Jack looked at her then, a puzzled, imploring look.

"You don't know what I mean."

"What do you mean?"—with a flicker of a smile.

He breathed deeply.

"I mean that I love you—that I want to marry you."

"That," said Amy, "is what I thought you meant."

Late that night, in his room at the hotel, Jack scribbled a note to David Lee and one to his mother. To Lee he wrote:

You needn't worry any longer about my dependability. I'm engaged to be married. . . . She's the kind of a girl who could no more understand my not being on the job than she could understand quitting of any kind. I'm going to work my head off. If it's in me at all, I'll be on Broadway in a year.

To his mother he wrote briefly that he was to be married, mentioning the girl's name, Amy Prentiss.

His letters brought two prompt results. David Lee offered him a part in the coming "Frivolities" and instructed him to leave for New York at once for rehearsals. And old Cantor Rabinowitz, not so strong as he used to be, had a nervous collapse.

"A *Shiksa!*" he repeated over and over as he lay in his bed. "A *Shiksa!* Our Jakie should marry a *Shiksa!* God in heaven, why do you let me live to suffer like this?"

His white-haired wife, broken-hearted, tried to console him.

"What could you tell it from a name, Yosele? A name, it ain't nothing. Look—our Jakie he goes by the name Jack Robin. Amy Prentiss—it could be she's a *Yiddishe* girl. Look—Jenny Levy from Ludlow Street is her name on the stage Genevieve Leeds. Wait we should hear from Jakie some more."

"It's a *Shiksa*," her husband insisted. "If it was a *Yiddishe* girl, he would have written it in the letter. I feel it—I know it—it's a *Shiksa*. *Gott im Himmel*, help me to live out my last years!"

The next Tuesday evening Jack came unexpectedly. As he stepped into the spotless little flat, his father, who was sitting before the kitchen table in his shirt-sleeves, a skullcap on his white head, reading loudly to himself from the *Mishna*, looked up mildly over his glasses and spoke the question he must have rehearsed scores of times to himself.

"To a *Shiksa* you're engaged, ain't it?"

Jack hesitated. The calmness of his father he sensed at once as being anything but indifference. He suddenly was swept with shame for not having thought more about what his engagement would mean to them.

The old man had turned back to the *Mishna*. Apparently, Jack's hesitation had replied adequately. And now his mother came into the kitchen from the narrow, dark corridor of the tenement. Jack kissed her wrinkled cheek. It was the first time in years that he had kissed her, and it thrilled the old woman. But in a moment she had observed the portentous absorption of her husband in his book of the Talmud.

"Yosele, don't you see our Jakie is here?"

The cantor continued with the low-murmured singsong as if he had not heard her. She turned to Jack, who gave her a queer smile and an almost imperceptible shrug of the shoulders.

"Then it's a *Shiksa*?" she whispered. Briskly she moved to the kitchen

159

stove. "You'll stay for supper, Jakie?" she asked over her shoulder. "Sit down. I'll have it quick ready. The soup is already on the stove—*Borsht*, red-beets soup, Jakie—and to-night we got it cucumbers in sour cream, and cheese *Blintzes*, too."

The old cantor joined them at the table, but beyond the various ritual prayers he and Jack mumbled together, he did not utter a word. The old woman, pathetically striving to eke out some harmony from the situation, made not the slightest attempt to get Jack to talk of his *fiancée*.

"You are coming to the synagogue next Sabbath?"

"I'm sorry, ma. I'm going to be terribly busy. You see, this is my one big chance. Lee has been fine, and it's up to me to repay him. He's one of these men who doesn't do things half-way. Either he backs you to the limit or he drops you. He's watching me closely, and I have to prove I can be relied upon. He's not giving me a star part, but I'm a principal, and if I make a hit, I'll rise fast with David Lee. This is the first time, ma, that my future has meant anything to me, and I'm going to give all I have to rehearsals."

When the meal was cleared off the table, the old cantor moved with his tome to the smaller kitchen table, where he went on with his low-toned recitative of the Talmud. Jack and his mother sat in silence at the larger table. Then Jack placed his hand tenderly over hers.

"Ma, it's a funny thing, but I'm just beginning to appreciate what you and pa mean to me. I never realized it until suddenly last week I—"

"Do you hear what our Jakie is saying, Yosele? He's saying that now he's grown up and he knows how good it is a papa and a mamma. He's saying—"

It was as if the old man had not heard.

They talked on softly, rapidly at first, exchanging ideas and comments, and then peaceful silences crept between them. After a rather long pause in the talk, his mother said, with a casual air:

"You know, Jakie, I was just thinking the other day—I was thinking that if a *Yiddishe* girl marries a *Goyisher* boy, then it's bad, because you know how it is in a house—everything is like the father wants. But if a *Yiddisher* boy marries a *Goyishe* girl, then it ain't so terrible. She could be learned to buy *Kosher* meat and to have two kinds of dishes, for *Fleischige* and for *Milchige*—and the children could be brought up like *Yiddishe* children; they could be sent to a *Chaidar*—I was just thinking like this only yesterday, Jakie. Ain't it funny I should think of it?"

Jack's hand tightened over hers.

"You're sweet, ma," he said slowly. "I'm afraid it can't be. I was brought up that way, ma, and I've been unhappy all my life. And Amy was brought up the other way, and she's been happy from the day she was a baby. I'll want my children to be happy like Amy is."

The sharp sound of a book snapping shut twisted their attention to the cantor. He had risen, and, eyes blazing, was pointing a shaking finger at Jack.

"Go out!" he cried. "Go out from my house—bum! Go!" A fit of coughing seized him, and he sank to his chair. They hastened to his side. The old man was unable to speak, but his eyes glared so that Jack stepped back. His mother turned, tragic-eyed, to him and said,

"Maybe you better go, Jakie."

There are few tasks more absorbing and exacting than that of rehearsing for the "Frivolities," and the days which followed for Jack were so full that he found time only to telephone his mother. As there was no connection directly to the flat on Hester Street, Jack had to call the drug store on the corner. He succeeded in getting her but twice in the five times he called. His father was well, she told him cheerfully, but naturally getting old and feeble. She doubted whether he would be able to continue as cantor for very many more years, but thanked God that he would be able to lead in the services for the coming holy day, Yom Kippur—the Day of Atonement. "Maybe you will come to the synagogue then, and fast the whole day?" she asked wistfully.

"Ma, I don't see how I can possibly come. It's the fifteenth, and our show opens on Broadway the same evening. I—I'd give anything, ma, to be able to come. I'd do it for my own sake as well as for papa's and yours. It's beginning to mean something to me—Yom Kippur. You see how it is, don't you, ma?"

"Yes," his mother sighed; "I see."

The second time, she brought up the subject again.

"Your papa he's ain't feeling so good, Jakie. Maybe this will be his last Yom Kippur. He talks about you. He is all the time talking about you. He says God has punished him enough for his sins that he should be the last Rabinowitz in ten generations to sing *Chazonoth* in a *Shool*. He don't *say* you should come on Yom Kippur—he didn't talk about that. But I think in his heart he means it, Jakie."

"I'll tell you what I'll do, ma," he replied, after some thought. "We open Monday night, and there probably will be a lot of changes made in the special rehearsal on Tuesday. But I'll try to dodge that Tuesday rehearsal and come to the synagogue for the morning and most of the afternoon."

"You're a good boy, Jakie."

Amy, who had swung West on the vaudeville circuit, was in Denver at this time. Jack wrote her every day—love-letters, almost childish in their outpouring of longing, full of high resolve, glowing with the miracle of the new insight he felt he was getting into life.

I realize that with me it isn't a question of ability, but of character. I've seen enough of this show to believe that I can put my songs over so big that Lee will have to star me. But I must be unswervingly steady. I have to be as good at the end of the season as on the opening night. I have to be on hand all of the time. My health must be guarded as well as my impulses. I don't even want to miss a performance with illness as an excuse. I can see that some of them are a bit leery of me—they're not dead-sure they can depend on me. Lee is the only one who's different. He's like a rock. I'd rather break a leg than fail him. But your wonderful confidence and my own resolution make me smile at them. I know I'll come through.

Swiftly the last month of rehearsal went by, and then the great day came. At two Monday afternoon, David Lee, who had attended the dress-rehearsal, called a halt.

"That's all," he said. "Take it easy until to-night. Robin, I want to see you."

He took Jack aside in a corner of the shadowy theatre.

"You're a winner if you can come through. Not exactly a world-beater—Frank Binney and Hal Bolton and Eddie Loren and Helen Kennedy still have something you haven't got. I don't know what it is, but you have the *capacity* to get it. I've seen it show suddenly in talented performers, sometimes overnight. But you'll make the electric lights, and I'm behind you. Now beat it, and be sure to take it easy."

At three in the afternoon, Jack, in his suite at the family hotel on Seventy-ninth Street, was busily writing a letter to Amy, who was in Salt Lake City. He had taken a hot bath, intending to sleep off some of his nervousness after this note to his sweetheart. He finished the letter and had just sunk beneath the covers of his bed when the telephone-bell rang. It was old Chiam Yudelson, friend and neighbor of his parents, to tell him that his father had just died.

When Jack's taxi-cab drew up before his home in Hester Street, a harassed policeman was swinging his club in the effort to disperse the crowd in front of the tenement where the beloved cantor lay dead. Jack elbowed his way through. He was recognized, and a pathway was instantly made for him.

In the tiny flat were his mother, the *Shamas* of the synagogue, old Chiam Yudelson and his wife, and Lawyer Feldman, the friend of all Hester Street. Greater perhaps than her grief at the loss of the man who had loved her and his God with equal fervor for sixty years was Mrs. Rabinowitz's panic at the thought that it was Yom Kippur eve and that the lyric voice of a Rabinowitz would not be raised in supplication to wipe out the sins of the Chosen People before their Creator. When Jack crowded his way through the friends and neighbors who packed the dark, narrow corridor, she was clinging to the hand of Lawyer Feldman.

"Look, Mr. Feldman," she was saying; "it's only two hours to Yom Kippur. It's got to be a good *Chazon* to sing. The last words my Yosele he said to me, he said, 'Rivka, get our Jakie.' So low he says it, Mr. Feldman, I couldn't hardly hear him. His face was white like a *Yahrzeit* candle, and he says to me: 'Rivka, God will forgive our Jakie if he will sing "*Kol Nidre*" for me to-night. Maybe my dying,' he says, 'will make a *Chazon* from our Jakie. Tell him, Rivka,' he says. Look, Mr. Feldman; Jakie is maybe coming here. Maybe you could talk to him. In his heart he's a good boy. Tell him—tell him—his father is dead—tell him—oh, Mr. Feldman, my heart is breaking in pieces—I—I can't talk no more—"

"Here's Jakie!" Chiam Yudelson broke in.

The next moment his mother was in his arms. Lawyer Feldman drew her gently away, and she turned into the other room—the bedroom where her dead husband lay. Silence followed. Nervously Jack went after her, fearing that silence.

It was an immaculately clean room—so clean that every rip in the wall-paper, every stain on the plastered ceiling stared at them, hollow-eyed, terrible in nakedness. The bed, a thing of iron tubing, whose green paint had long since scaled off, stood head against an ancient oak book-case, crammed with old-fashioned mahogany-colored books of the Talmud, the *Chumesh*, the various prayer-books, and a mass of huge music portfolios filled with note-scribbled sheets. On the bed lay his father's body. It had been covered completely with a white sheet, but his mother, flung across it, had drawn the sheet off so that the waxlike face and one thin old shoulder were revealed. Jack looked long at his father's face. It was beautiful in death. Every line in it spoke of a brave, poetic fight, of deep, fierce religious faith. His mother's body shuddered, and Jack reached over to take her hand.

She rose from the bed then, and son and mother stood alone.

"I—I came as soon as I—heard," Jack said.

His mother's hand rested lightly against his coat.

"He—he died this morning. It was a quarter to twelve. Yesterday he got sick. He talked about you—all the time about you, Jakie. At a quarter to twelve he died—a quarter to twelve. He just closed his eyes—like a baby, Jakie—and he said—he said: 'Rivka,' he said, 'God will forgive our Jakie if he will sing "*Kol Nidre*" for me to-night. Maybe,' he said, 'maybe—maybe—' Oh, Jakie, I—Jakie, *mein Kind*, your father is dead—I can't stand it—"

She was again in his arms. Lawyer Feldman appeared in the doorway.

"Better take her out of that room," he suggested. "It isn't doing her any good. Has she spoken to you about—"

Jack nodded. He gently led his mother toward the kitchen. As they passed him, the lawyer asked in a low tone,

"Are you going to do it?"

Jack placed his mother in a chair, where she sat blankly, looking first at the friends gathered in the kitchen, then out of the window where the crowds were still pushing and surging noisily, and then, in a most pathetic and forlorn way, down at her hands folded so helplessly in her lap.

The *Shamas*, who was there, mainly for the purpose of finding out whether Jack would serve as cantor that evening and the next day or whether he would have to step into the breach himself, was becoming nervous and impatient. He approached Jack, who looked unseeingly at him.

It was four-thirty. If he appeared in the show that evening, singing ragtime songs while his father lay dead—while the Hester Street Synagogue went cantorless for the first Day of Atonement in forty years—while his mother struggled under an unbearable double grief—

He turned to the *Shamas*.

"My father's *Talis*, it is at the synagogue?"

"Yes; everything is in the *Shool*, Mr. Rabinowitz," the *Shamas* replied eagerly.

"The tunes—the *Genigen*—of the choir—are they the same my father used ten, fifteen years ago?"

"The same *Genigen*, exactly."

"All right. I'll be there at six o'clock."

As Jack took his mother in his arms to sit out the next hour with her and to comfort her, the tears for the first time since her husband died flowed from her eyes, and she said over and over to him:

"In your heart you're a good boy. I always told him that in your heart you're a good boy."

News travels like lightning in the East Side. "Jack Robin—the vaudeville headliner—is singing as cantor at the Hester Street Synagogue this Yom Kippur!" It might have been a newspaper scare headline, for by six-thirty that evening the slowly arriving members of the Hester Street Synagogue congregation had almost to fight their way through the mob that packed the street up to the corners of both Norfolk and Essex Streets. Wealthy East Siders, who had paid their ten and twelve dollars for pews in the much larger Beth Medresh Hagadol, neglected that comparatively splendid house of prayer to stand in the crammed lobby of the Hester Street Synagogue and listen to the golden notes of this young singer of ragtime as he rendered *"Kol Nidre"* with a high, broken sobbing which, they insisted critically, surpassed his father's in his best days.

Every twist and turn of his father's had been branded unforgettably in Jack's memory from childhood days, but he sang the grief-laden notes with a lyric passion that was distinctly his own. The low-hanging rafters of the old synagogue, the cheap, shiny chandeliers of painted gold, the faded velvet hangings on the holy vault where the parchments of the Old Testament stood, the gold-fringed, worn white-silk cloth that covered the stand in the pulpit where he prayed—these called to something surging and powerful in him, something which made his whole life since his boyhood seem blurred and unreal.

When, with the congregation standing and swaying in humility before their Creator, he uttered that refrain which asks forgiveness for every sin of mankind from evil thoughts to murder, rising from a low sing-song into a quivering, majestic wail and then breaking into incoherent plaintiveness, the sobs choked his throat.

His mother sat in the small gallery at the back reserved for women, and he saw her when, after marching slowly forward with the choir, he had flung open the hangings before the holy vault and turned to face the congregation as he led in the appeal that the "prayers of this evening shall come before the Divine Presence in the morning and by nightfall bring redemption for all sins."

When he finished the high melodious strains of this triumphant yet humble and supplicating piece, there was a low murmur of approbation throughout the synagogue.

The rabbi, a rotund little man in the front pews, turned to his neighbor and remarked:

"Even Rosenblatt, when I heard him in Moscow, didn't give a *'Yaaleh'* like this. *Aza Singen nehmt by die Harz!"*

When the time came for *Kadish*, the prayer uttered only by those in mourning their dead, the whole congregation rose in silence in honor of the cantor who was dead and his son and wife. The other mourners subdued their customary loud recital, and the voices of Jack and his mother, the one flowing and resonant, the other high and broken with sobs, were heard clearly.

Crowds followed the couple as they slowly walked the half-block to the tenement-house that evening. As they paused on the stoop, Jack turned to the gathering people and in a low voice asked them to be good enough to leave his mother and himself alone with their grief. Instantly a cry was raised:

"Beat it!"

"Go home, bums, loafers! Ain't you got no respect for the *Chazon*?"

"G'wan! Can't you leave some peace be even on Yom Kippur—*Paskudniks*!"

The crowd dispersed.

Jack sat up until midnight that night with his mother, and then, completely weary, he fell asleep, to dream fitfully of Amy and of David Lee, of David Lee and of Amy, until morning.

David Lee slept fitfully also that night. Jack's failure at the last moment to appear on the opening night had ruined three numbers and had made two others awkward, and Lee had a difficult job ahead of him in the next twenty-four hours. He wasted no time thinking about the delinquent. "*He's* going to do the worrying, not me," he said grimly to Harry Anthony. He stayed up until four in the morning, telephoning and telegraphing in the effort to get a substitute so much better than Jack that the reviews of Tuesday, probably derogatory, would be reversed on Wednesday morning.

His efforts did not meet with success, and he left word with his man to wake him early Tuesday. When his man called him, he asked for the morning papers.

He was about to turn to the theatrical page, when his eye was caught by a headline on the front sheet. Sitting on the edge of the bed, he read, and, as he read, a low whistle escaped him. He dropped the first paper and took another. He swore softly.

"That damn kid!" he murmured gleefully. "That damn kid! Stevens, tell Herman to have the car out in a half-hour."

He had to slip a crisp green bank-note into the hand of the policeman before room was made for him to stand in the crush in the narrow lobby of the Hester Street Synagogue. Jack Robin, swathed in the folds of a great black-striped linen *Talis*, an elaborate and stiff black-plush skull-cap on his head, his thin, handsome face deadly white, his dark eyes afire, was singing that splendid aria of his father's—"*Hamelech*," "The King"—and as the majesty of it rolled forth, broke, and narrowed into rivulets of humility, David Lee pinched himself to see if he were asleep.

Then, after a few moments of quick rattling recitative, Jack went on into a clear, low-toned series of sound which had the effect of musical talking, of superbly self-contained remonstrance. This speech gradually rose to a fluttering uncertainty, a bewildered pleading, and then the climax came—a flood of confession.

Excitedly Lee elbowed his way out of the crowd.

"Where's the nearest telephone?" he asked the policeman.

"Right on the corner—the drug store, sir."

In five minutes Harry Anthony was on the wire.

"Harry," said Lee, "do you want to hear the greatest ragtime singer in America in the making? A wonder, Harry, a wonder! Got Hal Bolton mopped off the boards. Come down right away. It's a dirty little hole down on the East Side called the Hester Street Synagogue. I'll meet you on the corner of Hester and Norfolk."

Appendix 3

Warner Brothers Studios

They say that anything will grow in the wonderful climate of Southern California, and the Warner Brothers studio lot on Sunset Boulevard, Hollywood, is a splendid confirmation of that statement. The Warners took over the land in 1918, when their increasing prosperity made a change in locale necessary. The thirteen-acre plot was desirable in point of location, conformation and utility, but thirteen acres was a lot of land, and had an earthquake come along about then the one puny building would have rattled around the lot like a pea in a peck measure. "Doc" Salmon, recruited from the Warner sales department in San Francisco to be studio superintendent, was also the property man, office boy, janitor and even on occasion the night watchman. The studio was a small two-stage affair, with electrical equipment barely sufficient to provide the necessary current. Today Salmon is overlord of more than 700 employees, and if he is around the studio nights, as he often is, it is only because the daylight hours are not long enough to permit him to crowd his multitude of details into the average working day.

And Frank Murphy, who had to stand over his dynamos with a whip when both stages were working, has charge of a plant about the size of that required for a city of 15,000 persons, in addition to a battery of portable generators that supply the lights for night work on location, when they are not being used for some important theatre opening. In the past year these lights have been loaned to twenty-five theatres. The value of the electrical equipment is upward of $750,000, and Murphy is still in charge.

Current is also supplied by this plant for the Warner broadcasting station KFWB, the tall aerials of which form one of the night and day landmarks of the film city.

The stages are lighted by the usual combination of Kleigs, Cooper-Hewitts, Lake tubes and various forms of carbon lights, and some idea of

Moving Picture World, March 26, 1927, pp. 394, 442–43. © 1927 Quigley Publications. Reprinted by permission.

the equipment may be gained from the fact that last year the studio used more than 100,000 carbons. Lay them end to end for yourself if you wish.

The first stage was built in 1922 with dimensions 325 by 145 feet, which made it one of the largest stages in the world at that time. Today the original stage has three duplicates, each of about the same floor space.

The original thirteen acres have not been expanded, for expansion is not necessary, and ingenious planning has made the space ample, but when Warners bought out Vitagraph two years ago, they acquired a 23-acre plot, fully equipped by A. E. Smith, one of the oldest producers in the business. This lot is now used for overflow work.

R. Louis Geib started with Warners in 1918 as Technical Director, but he had no one to direct, since he had no permanent helpers in his department. He not only designed the sets, but he helped to build and erect them, painted them, dressed them, kept them clean, and finally tore them down. He was a thoroughly practical builder, for in addition to six years on the Fox lot as carpenter he was a building contractor on the side. He has no time for side issues today, for he is in command of a woodworking shop with equipment costing $15,000, a machine shop with $20,000 worth of equipment which not only builds for production but keeps the cameras and laboratory machinery in repair, and also has charge of other machine equipment, valued at about $15,000.

With the collaboration of Esdras Hartley, the art director, he has laid out the building plan of the lot, and takes pride in the contention that it is the cleanest and most compact studio lot on the coast.

They also designed and built the fireproof laboratory, which is a model of compactness and efficiency. It has not lost a day since its opening, either for repairs or lack of work.

As a sample of what they can do, it may be mentioned that recently there were in production in this 13-acre space seven features, "Bitter Apples," "The Gay Old Bird," "A Million Bid," "What Every Girl Should Know," "Hills of Kentucky," "Matinee Ladies," and "White Flannels," and still the units did not intrude on each other.

All properties and costumes are made on the lot. The property room occupies a part of the building erected in the exact center of the property, originally occupied by the "old" stage, as distinguished from the "Number One" which came in 1922. This is a modern three-story building of 24,000 square feet of floor space containing the offices of the Studio Manager, Publicity, Technical and Art Departments, the office of the Studio Superintendent, Transportation Department and timekeepers in addition to the property room.

The property room is in charge of Albert C. ("Whitey") Wilson, who came to Warners three and a half years ago to take charge of the then very small collection. Today the stock in his care is valued at $400,000 and includes 15,000 numbered pieces of property, 3,200 drapes and about 1,400 pieces of electrical fixtures. One single purchase of antique and art objects amounted to $60,000, and Whitey made a special trip to New York to pick precisely what he wanted from recent importations. This stock includes the properties obtained from the Vitagraph purchase. After furnishings and drapes have been used a few times, they are sold to make room for fresh purchases that the dressings of the sets may not become trade marks.

Much of the material is produced in the various mechanical departments, such as the furniture, cabinet, paint, machine, stone and electrical shops and little has to be purchased or rented. A recent achievement was the rounding up of prehistoric automobiles for "The First Automobile." Hollywood could produce but four of the earliest types of cars. Doc Salmon directed a combing of Southern California and made the picture with eleven "museum pieces" ranging from 26 to 28 years of age. The chief rental item, however, is animals, for it is the Warner policy to keep no animals on the lot.

John L. Warner is in personal charge of production, and presides over a production cabinet composed of Darryl Zanuck, associate executive; William Koenig, studio manager; Louis Geib, technical director; Doc Salmon, general superintendent; Esdras Hartley, chief architect; Harold McCord, editor, and Whitey Wilson, master of properties.

Each spring Mr. Warner comes East to consult with his brothers, Harry M., Albert and Sam Warner, regarding the campaign for the season. For the season now waning it was planned to make a series of 26 features and six specials at a cost of $14,000,000.

On his return to Hollywood consultations were initiated and the production schedule mapped out, which has been followed with little difficulty. The scripts were given to the members of the studio staff best qualified to handle that type of story, and special writers were hired where it was felt that they could do the work better.

The policy is to make the better-than-program picture, and it is Mr. Warner's belief that the special of today will be the program standard of the coming years.

The Warner stars include many real stars. Syd Chaplin, who has at last worked himself out of the eclipse of his more famous brother's name, has done splendid work since he came under the Warner Brothers, and the beautiful and talented Dolores Costello owes to them a majority of her best roles. Monte Blue is a long-time favorite, and Irene Rich needs no special comment. Louise Fazenda supplies much of the comedy and Patsy Ruth Miller excels in modern roles. May McAvoy has lately been added to the stock, and Jason Robards, a comparative newcomer, is rapidly gaining fame. Myrna Loy is another new name, but William Demarest brings with him his dramatic and vaudeville repute. Helen Costello and Leila Hyams are two baby stars who are rapidly outgrowing their swaddling clothes.

The scripts are developed by the scenarists under Darryl Zanuck, and include Graham Baker, Harvey Gates, Anthony Coldeway, Johnnie Grey, Tom Gibson and Bryan Foy.

As soon as the scenarists have begun their tasks, Frank Kingsley and his assistant, George Leonard Taylor, begin to cast the production. Both are experts in their line, and while their work has been simplified by the Central Casting Bureau, theirs is no sinecure.

Among the directors the chief are James Flood, Walter Morosco, Charles Reisner, Monte Bell, Howard Bretherton, who graduated from the film cutting ranks; Byron Haskins and Ray Enright, also a former cutter.

Included in the assistant directors are Henry Blanke, Ross Lederman, Sandy Roth, Gordon Hollingshead, Ted Stevens, Eddie Sowders, William Cannon and George Webster.

Both directors and assistants are supplemented by special engagements, but these are the standing army.

Among the cameramen on the lot are Ed du Parr, who did the unusually good photography for "The Better 'Ole." Following that production he was brought to New York for special instruction in Vitaphone technic, and will have charge of the camera work done on Vitaphone for the western studio. Others are Dave Abel, Nelson Laraby, Akeley and stunt camera man, who puts the thrills on record; Virgil Miller, Hal Mohr, and Al Nicklun, the latter in charge of equipment and the titling cameras. All of them are men of long experience and highly developed technical knowledge.

Probably no department is more important than the cutting room, and it is from here that many of the best directors have emerged. The experience the men get from cutting and trimming the rushes and assembling them for final selection gives them a sense of scene and story values that is even better training than the more active service of the assistant directors.

Following the usual system, the positive goes to the cutter, who trims and assembles, day by day, following the story sequence, until the complete product is assembled. By the time the shooting is done there will be from 12 to 30 reels; much of it duplicate, but still enough original matter to require expert handling to get it into the final five to seven or eight reels.

The director sits in with suggestions, and is consulted on changes in the continuity or rearrangement of scenes which the editor has reason to believe will tense up the action or give better contrast. When the final cutting and titling has been done, the picture is taken to some theatre to give the editor an opportunity to sense the audience reaction and sometimes there may be one or two more, each followed by changes in the cutting and titling, before the completed picture is shipped to New York and the editor turns his attention to the next job.

Harold McCord is head of the editing department and personally has cut "Don Juan," "When a Man Loves," "Millionaires," "Finger Prints" and "A Million Bid."

Clarence Kolster is chief aide, and cuts from six to eight pictures a year. Charles Henckel is another fast worker and Ray Enright has cut most of the Syd Chaplin comedies, and did so well that he has been promoted to a directorship. Howard Bretherton is another to drop the shears and cement brush for the megaphone.

Title writing is another of the fine arts too little appreciated, and the ideal aimed at in the Warner title department is to make the titles fitting companions to the pictured action and yet so inconspicuous that the spectator carries with him no vital memory of the titles. The Warner policy is to regard the title as a general detriment to the action, and to make interruption only where it is necessary to explain the action or account for a lapse of time.

There are instances, however, where the use of a subtitle not only explains an action, but has a dramatic value peculiarly its own. One example of this is to be found in "Clash of the Wolves" in which Rin-Tin-Tin is supposed to run a cactus thorn into his paw. To picture this action, particularly in a close-up, as would have been necessary, would have aroused a resentful sympathy for the animal that would have reacted against the production. A subtitle with a drawn design of the foot coming down forcefully on the thorn was used instead. The drawing did not offend. It created the proper understanding, and no one wrote letters to the newspapers calling upon the S.P.C.A. to do its stuff.

From another angle, in "Three Weeks in Paris," it was pointed out, when the film was ready for release, that scenes were shown in the interior of the Opera House, but the exterior of the building was not shown.

Instead of lengthening the film with a library shot of the Paris Grand Opera, the titles for this sequence were redrawn with a picture of the building. It worked even better than the cut-in, and held the picture down to length.

The art work in the titles is done on black card with various shades of grey pastel, and the title cards are painted in white on black cards by a special process.

Last year all main titles were hand lettered in a uniform script. This season a change has been made to an individual lettering for each title, suggested wherever possible, by the title itself, as in "Across the Pacific" in which the lettering ingeniously suggests a wave effect.

Where possible the titles are taken from the original script, but it is more often found that these can be improved upon when viewed in connection with the actual action and they either are changed or completely replaced.

The title writer is a specialist in his line and often is able to suggest material improvements, and always he thinks of titles in terms of audience comprehension where the original script writer is more apt to consider only the literary values.

Robert Hopkins is the title writer on the Warner lot and personally had titled a majority of the product. However such experts as Rupert Hughes, Don Ryan and Walter Anthony have been called in to assist when the pressure exceeded the one-man capacity.

Fifteen years ago the editor, who in those days was also the advertising man and publicity writer, felt that the gods indeed had been kind if he could coax a half dozen stills from the cameramen on a one-reel release. And if one of those six could be worked into a really good cut, his cup of bliss overflowed. In those days the cinematographer was provided with a still camera, generally a 5 by 7, and when he remembered to take it out of its carrying case, he would shoot the deadest part of the scene. Contrast this with the set of 600 8 by 10 stills made during the filming of "Don Juan," and the equal number for "The Better 'Ole." Even on the less elaborate productions the number never runs below 100 and is often more. In addition each set is photographed before it is used and again before it is torn down, for the convenience of the technical department should any emergency require its rebuild.

Each Warner unit has its own still cameraman who is trained to a sense of what is and is not good material for reproduction. In addition he makes the "portrait stills" of the players as they appear in that particular production, and aids in the making of "production stills," which are stills made during the production rather than of it. Many of these portray the difficulties or the humorous incidents during the filming of a picture, may show special devices or merely show the routine of production. There is a large demand for these from fan magazines, the daily and weekly papers and the trade publications. A second class of production stills are those showing the home life of the stars. On the Warner lot they even photograph the properties.

Things certainly do sprout in California—when they are properly irrigated. Back in 1918 the Warner lot boasted one building, employed an average of 75 persons and paid them approximately $1,200 a week. Today the entire thirteen acres are neatly and compactly studded with buildings and the cashier pays out around $150,000 a week to some 700 employees. Evidently the salaries have grown, along with other things, in that well-advertised climate.

Appendix 4

Vitaphone Activity in Hollywood

By Edwin Schallert

The first Vitaphone films have been made in Hollywood. They are short subjects—a preliminary to the first big test of this sound-recording innovation with the production of "The Jazz Singer," starring Al Jolson.

One can survey the results of the experiments and the benefits accruing from the establishing of a Vitaphone studio in the picture-producing center—benefits that will undoubtedly prove very important for this innovation combining sound with motion pictures.

Warner Brothers already have two stages in operation, and two more under way on their property on Sunset Boulevard. The stages are soundproof construction. They are of moderate size. They possess many advantages over the equipment of the Manhattan Opera House in New York, where all Vitaphonized pictures have been made heretofore.

Warner Brothers are to try a new line of experiments, particularly for "The Jazz Singer." They are planning to use dialogue in certain scenes of this production—dialogue with musical accompaniment. Al Jolson will sing jazz songs, and in the culminating episode the famous "Kol Nidrei [sic]."

The effectiveness of this culminating episode hinges, of course, upon the celebrated Jewish chant. Jolson as a stage star in the plot renews the call of blood, and takes the place of his dying father, a cantor, in the synagogue. There was a deep appeal to this denouement on the stage. It is hoped to preserve this on the screen through the Vitaphone.

I watched two of the Vitaphone prologues in the making. One was called "A Night at Coffee Dan's," an impression of an evening of entertainment in a famous San Francisco resort. The other was a Spanish-California atmospheric act, designed to be used with the picture "Old San Francisco."

Motion Picture News, July 8, 1927, pp. 35–36. © 1927 Quigley Publications. Reprinted by permission.

There are very definite purposes behind the production of these Vitaphone acts. First of all they are to serve as a new form of embellishment on picture programs, wherever it is possible to use them, and this means wherever Vitaphone is installed in a theatre. Second, they are planned to develop the Vitaphone technique, especially along photographic lines, which so far have been somewhat deficient—to make Vitaphone productions truly productions in a pictorial sense. Thirdly, it is felt that they may lead to the discovery of much new talent, particularly among those who have had camera experience. All this is preparatory to the production of Vitaphone features like "The Jazz Singer."

Warner Brothers now have a projection room that is equipped with Vitaphone. Records are played here frequently even during the running of the daily rushes. It serves to relieve the monotony, and gives to a degree, at least, the feeling of a theatre presentation.

In this projection room I saw one day a test Vitaphone film that had been made with Buster Collier. He did a song number, and evidenced a surprisingly good voice. What interested me more, however, was his demeanor before the camera. He had an ease of manner that was missing in the case of the majority of Vitaphone performers that I had seen previously. He was camera wise. The result was salutary. It took away the stiffness that is characteristic of many Vitaphone performances, and if anything the voice as it came through the loudspeaker possessed a new reality. I think this was because the action coordinated more satisfactorily.

For the novelty of it, I took part in a Vitaphone scene as atmosphere one day, and can look back on this as a very unique experience. Relating it may be of interest to the readers of Motion Picture News, because so little has been told as yet of Vitaphone film-making.

The stage on which the company worked was, as I have indicated, somewhat smaller than those to which one usually is accustomed nowadays in Hollywood. The walls were covered with sound-proof felt-like paper. Otherwise the general construction was not unusual.

Various other differences were, however, to be noted in the equipment. One of these differences was a glass-enclosed compartment, with a sort of bay-window effect, projecting from one of the sidewalls at some height from the floor. Still another was a movable sound-proof booth enclosing the camera [see figure 26].

The compartment projecting from the wall, I learned upon inquiry, contained the recording apparatus, and was called the "mixer." The name originates from the fact that oftentimes the waves of sound are received from two different sources, namely two different microphones, and that the volume from each of these has to be separately regulated—thus "mixed" or blended. It could, of course, be received from even more than two microphones, but that is the number now ordinarily used.

In the scene in which I took part the orchestra was not photographed but played behind a curtain, and the music which they rendered was recorded in a different microphone from that which caught the voices of the singers in a cabaret scene on which the camera was focused. The orchestra had to be toned down perhaps a trifle to combine correctly with the singing. It would have crowded the picture to have photographed them in the scene, and it is doubtful if they would have added anything to its pictorial interest. Hence the reason for having them play off scene.

Lighting arrangements differ materially on the Vitaphone set from those on the ordinary set. At times, incandescents are used exclusively—very bright ones—this being an innovation. In some experiments these incandescents have been supplemented by mercury bank lights, but lamps that have to be trimmed noisily cannot be used. Even the bank lights that are adjacent to the microphone have to be shut off occasionally because of their humming, so sensitive is the recording apparatus to every slight noise.

Vitaphone recording has to be done continuously. A performance has to last at least six minutes. It is preferable perhaps for it to run six minutes or multiples of six, like twelve or eighteen, but it can run somewhat less or more than these multiples.

The act must be routined thoroughly so that there are no halts in its progress. The film is made in special lengths even up to 1000 feet, and consequently the camera magazines are about twice the normal size.

A scene that runs as much as 150 feet in the ordinary process of film-making is, of course, a rarity. This means a little over two minutes. The Vitaphone scene in which I worked lasted nine.

Everything has to be silent on the set as the recording starts. The effect is uncannily like that at a prayer-meeting or spiritualistic seance. There are no directions issued except possibly by hand motion once a scene is started. There is a moment of silence after it is finished. This is so no noise extraneous to the performance will intrude. Even a whisper is recorded.

Vitaphone is a very sensitive contrivance but not so difficult to regulate as it might seem. The recording and photographing moved smoothly while I was on the set, and I spent nearly a day there on one occasion. There was only one halt in the action when the film broke, and the act then had to be carried through from the beginning.

There is one decided advantage over the motion picture in sound recording. The record can be played back immediately. Two impressions are made for this purpose in wax. One of these is preserved for the matrix from which the final hard record is moulded. The other record is played, and, of course, is destroyed in the process. This enables some estimate to be made of the performance without delay, whereas the film requires a day at least for developing and printing.

The Vitaphone prologue for "Old San Francisco" showed the possibilities pictorially that may be arrived at with a stage properly equipped as regards photography. Even though short, I imagine it will prove quite effective. The setting was a plaza in front of an old Mission, the company being garbed in romantic and picturesque costumes suggesting early Spanish California.

There was chorus singing off stage by a choir. This was followed by a vocal solo by Sam Ash, formerly with "Rose-Marie" company, and a dance by Lina Basquette, former child star at Universal, and now the wife of S. L. Warner, who is in charge of the Vitaphone productions. The act closed with excerpts from "Carmen" and a march of the soldiers in brilliant Spanish uniforms, and playing trumpets and other brass instruments, while those taking part in the fiesta joined the procession.

Eddie Peabody, who has been a favorite at the Metropolitan Theatre in Los Angeles, famous for his banjo-playing, has also made a record, and there is another called the Pullman Porter act. These were all turned out in the course of a few weeks, directed by Bryan Foy, the son of Eddie Foy, and it is apparent that there will be no handicaps interfering with ample production.

The future of Vitaphone, with the new scope of activities, offers much food for interesting speculation. I noted among film salesmen who visited recent conventions on the Coast that there was much interest in and conversation about the experiments in the brief reproduction of sound with pictures. This took in Movietone as well as Vitaphone, and the belief was expressed by many visiting delegates that all the larger companies would eventually become interested in one or the other of these devices.

During conversation with Sam Warner, he mentioned that the number of installations totaled 135—this being several weeks ago—and that Vitaphone was being installed in theatres at a very rapid rate now.

For the most part this equipment will be used in the smaller theatres later, which are regarded as a most promising field for Vitaphone and other sound-producing inventions. It seems pretty well conceded that these devices eventually will become a necessary adjunct of every theatre's equipment—not for continuous use, but as the occasion and opportunity arise.

It goes without saying that Jolson's association with Vitaphone will greatly stimulate its future. "The Jazz Singer" will also test, if only perhaps in a rudimentary way, the idea of talking pictures. There will be no attempt as yet to treat a motion picture as a spoken drama; what dialogue there is in "The Jazz Singer" will probably be purely incidental, and as previously stated will be accompanied by music. This is a deft innovation. The scenes in which it will be used will probably be those between Jolson and his father. It will indeed be an accomplishment to have a permanent record of the voice and personality of one of the stage's great comedians. For this reason, it may be taken for granted that "The Jazz Singer" will be a very elaborate production.

There would seem to be a great chance with Vitaphone to bring to the screen grand opera, comic opera and musical shows. This is the eventual goal sought in the enterprise. Probably this sort of entertainment will be produced at first in tabloid form. Later on full-length productions will be made. However, this is well in the future.

Like the films the Vitaphone has an advantage over the stage. It can present a singer when he is in the best of voice, and can retake any other type of performance until the necessary perfection has been attained. It is not subject to casual influences and changing conditions, as is the performance in the flesh, any more than the motion picture itself is. This means much for its future.

Warner Brothers are staking much on the present Vitaphone experiments. They are investing $300,000 to $400,000 in equipment at their Coast studio, stages, laboratories, etc. They are into the game with a vengeance, and have already made very striking headway in a field in which they primarily are pioneering.

Appendix 5

How the Vitaphone Enters In

Alan Crosland, Warner Brothers' director, who is now filming "The Jazz Singer," starring Al Jolson in the title role, recently explained the details of the method by which full Vitaphone vocal numbers will be introduced for the first time into the action of a photoplay.

To begin with, it must be borne in mind that one reel of film is accompanied by just one sound record. The film can be cut, rearranged, shortened or anything desired—when not accompanied by Vitaphone—but since the record cannot be altered, once a thousand feet of film has been synchronized with a disk it must remain in precisely that form and length.

This means that if a "talking movie" throughout were being made it would be necessary to film a thousand feet at a time, synchronized with the record of the voices and used in just that form. Such is not the case with "The Jazz Singer," however. Songs will be introduced only at those points where they come in naturally and there will be no talking.

In Reel One, for instance, three songs are to be Vitaphoned in at three different points. During the other portions of the reel there will be a synchronized orchestral score. The method which Crosland will have to employ in filming is this:

First, all those portions of the reel which do not call for singing will be filmed. Then the reel will be assembled and cut, titles and all. The singing scenes will have been carefully rehearsed and timed to the second, and in the places in the reel where these are to go, blank film of an equivalent length will be placed.

Then, in the Vitaphone studio sets will be erected side by side for all three singing scenes. In the corner will be placed the accompanying orchestra for the picture with the projection machine to run it off, as is usual in "scoring" a picture for Vitaphone accompaniment. There will be four microphone circuits—one for each of the three sets and one for the orchestra.

New York Times, August 28, 1927, VII:4. © 1927 by The New York Times Company. Reprinted by permission.

When all is in readiness, the projection of the incomplete reel will start with the leader conducting the orchestra in the synchronized score which will be picked up by the first microphone. At the instant when the blank film flashes on the screen indicating the place for the first singing scene the orchestra will stop, and the microphone on the first set will be switched on while the first scene is recorded. As it comes to an end, one of the scenes previously filmed will flash on the orchestra's screen and the orchestra will resume the score. This process will be repeated for the second and third vocal numbers. All three sets must be lighted and ready, the timing must be perfect, and the players must be ready to make quick changes while the orchestra scores intervening scenes.

Appendix 6

Musical Score for "The Jazz Singer"

The following is a complete record of the musical score, as it appears in the studio files:

	Composition	Composer	Publisher	No. Bars
1.	Original	Silvers	Original Arrang.	13
2.	Russian Cradle Song	Krein	Belwin	12
3.	East Side, West Side	Lawlor	Orig. Arrangement	16
4.	Symphonie Espagnole	Lalo	" "	9
5.	Serenade Melancholique	Tschaikowski	" "	16
6.	Good Old Summertime	Evans	" "	14
7.	My Gal Sal	Dresser	Robbins	32
8.	Reves et Chimerie		Manus	44
9.	Robt. E. Lee	Muir	Robbins	20
10.	Reves et Chimerie		Manus	12
11.	Romeo & Juliet	Tschaikowski	Orig. Arrangement	25
12.	Serenade Melancholique	Tschaikowski	" "	12
13.	Original	Silvers	" "	22
14.	Souffrir et Mourir	Perfignan	Manus	12
15.	Symphonie Espagnole	Lalo	Orig. Arrangement	23
16.	Kol Nidre		Vitaphone	
17.	Hop Skip	Cohn	Berlin	15
18.	Mammy	Donaldson	Waterson	8
19.	Hop Skip	Cohn	Berlin	31
20.	Dirty Hands	Monoco	(Clark Leslie) Vitaphone	
21.	Toot Toot Tootsie	Fiorito	Feist-Vitaphone	
22.	I'm Lonely Without You	Green	Shapiro-Bernstein	46
23.	If A Girl Like You	Edwards	Mills	38
24.	Russian Cradle Song	Krein	Belwin	15
25.	Melodic Agitato	Savino	Robbins	71
26.	Serenade Melancholique	Tschaikowski	Orig. Arrangement	14
27.	Stray Sunbeams	Huerter	Schirmer	35
28.	If A Girl Like You	Edwards	Mills	92
29.	Yorzheit	Silberta	Vitaphone	
30.	If A Girl Like You	Edwards	Mills	28
31.	The Scandal Mongers		Belwin	40
32.	Humoresque	Tschaikowski	Orig. Arrangement	4
33.	Give My Regards to Bdwy.	Cohan	Fischer	32
34.	Humoresque	Tschaikowski	Orig. Arrangement	4
35.	Give My Regards to Bdwy.	Cohan	Fischer	14
36.	Yosel	Casman	Orig. Arrang. (Marks)	24
37.	Bar Kochba		Original	64
38.	Melodic Agitato	Savino	Robbins	32

Composition	Composer	Publisher	No. Bars
39. Original	Silvers	Orig. Arrangement	19
40. Mother Song	Silvers-Jolson	Orig. Arrangement	23
41. Prelude	Savino	Robbins	17
42. Prelude	Savino	Robbins	24
*			
48. Romeo & Juliet	Tschaikowski	Orig. Arrangement	25
49. La Foret Perfide	Gabriel-Marie	Manus	28
50. Original	Silvers	Orig. Arrangement	
51. Stray Sunbeams	Huerter	Schirmer	68
52. If A Girl Like You	Edwards	Mills	28
53. Stray Sunbeams	Huerter	Schirmer	17
54. Symphonie Espagnole	Lalo	Orig. Arrangement	30
55. Katinka	Friml	Schirmer	75
56. Bar Kochba		Orig. Arrangement	34
57. Chassidic Dance	Unknown	Fischer	19
58. Melodic Agitato	Savino	Robbins	28
59. Symphonie Espagnole	Lalo	Orig. Arrangement	23
60. Prelude	Savino	Robbins	26
61. Prelude	Savino	Robbins	22
62. Melodic Agitato	Savino	Robbins	28
63. At Evening	De Bussy	Orig. Arrangement	41
64. Chassidic Dance	Unknown	Fischer	35
65. Bar Kochba		Orig. Arrangement	15
66. Katinka	Friml	Schirmer	32
67. Prelude	Savino	Robbins	33
68. Mammy	Donaldson	Waterson	10
69. Melisande	Sibelius	Belwin	44
70. Kol Nidre	Unknown	Orig. Arrangement	4
71. Melisande	Sibelius	Belwin	55
72. Serenade Melancholique	Tschaikowski	Orig. Arrangement	48
73. Souffrir et Mourir	Perpignan	Manus	43
74. Katinka	Friml	Schirmer	15
75. Mother Song	Jolson-Silvers	Orig. Arrangement	15
76. Mother Song	Jolson-Silvers	Orig. Arrangement	32
77. Original	Silvers	Orig. Arrangement	23
78. Serenade Melancholique	Tschaikowski	Orig. Arrangement	23
79. At Evening	De Bussy	Orig. Arrangement	50
80. Souffrir et Mourir	Perpignan	Manus	39
81. Original	Silvers	Orig. Arrangement	41
82. Symphonie Espagnole	Lalo	Orig. Arrangement	38
83. Original	Silvers	Orig. Arrangement	13
84. Kol Nidre	Unknown	Vitaphone	
85. Mammy	Donaldson	Vitaphone	
Blue Skies	Berlin	Vitaphone	

*"It All Depends on You" and material unknown were originally recorded to appear at this point; "Blue Skies" was substituted later.

Appendix 7

"Vitaphone": What the Projection Entails

By P. H. Griffiths

In the Vitaphone system of making "talking pictures," the recording of the sound is done on a disc very similar to the ordinary gramophone record, except that the needle moves from the centre to the exterior both during recording and whilst projection is taking place. The reason for this is that the electrically operated stylus with which the record is made "tracks" better on the wax disc and thus enables better results to be obtained.

The Stroboscope

Synchronisation between the camera speed and that of the sound disc is attained by the use of special synchronous motors operated on one electric circuit.

The Bioscope Service Supplement, September 26, 1928, pp. xi–xii.

John Mullin of Santa Barbara, California, a specialist in the coming of sound, contributes the following corrections and notes:

"In the first paragraph the reason given for inside to outside tracking of the disc is erroneous. The reproducer, as in all record systems of the time, excluding Edison's Diamond Disc, used steel needles. A new needle with a sharp point could reproduce the inner diameter recorded material very satisfactorily at the low speed the groove traveled. As the needle point wore away during the playing of the record the velocity of the groove increased because outer grooves, at a larger diameter, naturally travel faster than inner grooves. The needle was therefore able to satisfactorily reproduce the sound throughout the entire playing time of the disc (from nine to eleven minutes). The needle was then thrown away and a fresh needle used for the next disc to be reproduced. Furthermore, the discs used in theaters were not made of wax. They were shellac pressings, exactly the same material as the old familiar 78 rpm phonograph records. Wax was used in the studio for cutting the master records. In the fourth paragraph under 'Speed' the record size is indicated as eighteen inches in diameter. It was not. It was sixteen inches. The amplifiers described were the very earliest employed and did not gain general acceptance."

Naturally certain precautions have to be taken to ensure perfect recording, but there is nothing of outstanding interest in them, with the exception of the stroboscope, as the device used to check synchronisation is called.

In one case, this takes the form of a disc two and a half inches in diameter, attached to the camera-driving mechanism and divided into segments coloured alternately black and white. A neon tube, connected to the same alternating current as the camera and turntable motors, illuminates these segments. The light from the neon tube fluctuates in accord with the alternating current, and, though these fluctuations are invisible to the naked eye, their effect is such that, when synchronisation is perfect, the disc of the stroboscope appears to be stationary. Another form of stroboscope is to have the edge of the turntable divided into black and white segments instead of having a special disc for this purpose.

The exhibitor, and his operators, are, however, far more concerned with the manner in which the picture and its sound accompaniment is projected than with the method of its recording, and, therefore, the particulars that follow should be found of interest.

"Vitaphone" Reproduction

Now for a rapid review of how reproduction is accomplished. There is the projector of standard type coupled to the turntable mechanism [see figure 28]. The film used in "Vitaphone" presentations is exactly the same as the ordinary film except that it has one "frame" or picture at the beginning specially marked with the word "START"—the film is threaded and run slowly through the projector till this "frame" covers the aperture, the record carrying the speech or music is set on the turntable and the reproducer "needle" placed on the starting point on the record which is indicated by an arrow. At the proper cue the motor driving both turntable mechanism and projector is switched in circuit starting both sound record and picture record off at the same moment.

The film is projected in the ordinary manner, while the speech or music is picked up from the record by the electrical reproducer that gives out a small electric current carrying the sound waves. This current passes to the amplifiers, is greatly reinforced and passes to the receivers and horns located near the screen where it is converted into sound.

Synchronisation

In a system of this kind it is essential that the sound and picture be in perfect synchronisation—that is to say, that the sound must be heard at the same instant that the action accompanying it is seen upon the screen. This is accomplished by having both turntable and projector operated by the same motor so that if the film and record are started simultaneously it necessarily follows that they will keep in step throughout.

A continuous programme can be obtained in the usual manner with the use of two projectors and turntables, changing over from one reel and its accompanying record to the following reel and record on the next projector.

Nothing to Worry About

There is nothing for the projectionist to get concerned over, for the equipment once installed—this is attended to by experts—needs little attention except for the charging of the batteries, and general maintenance, and attention to instructions, starting, stopping and change-over cues on both film and record.

Equipment

No special type or make of projector is necessary for the adaptation of "Vitaphone" equipment. A single specially designed motor drives both projector and turntable mechanism, and is operated on a special circuit by means of which the speed of the motor is maintained at 1,200 r.p.m. It is mounted on a substantial base supported by three telescoping legs by means of which its height may be adjusted; the motor control circuit is encased in a metal cabinet, and is connected to the motor by a multi-conductor cable. A special type of gear-box is situated forward of the driving motor upon the same table or base and is directly coupled to the motor shaft. The drive is transmitted from the motor through the gear-box and thence to projector mechanism by means of a vertical adjustable shaft fitted with universal joints at the mechanism end of which it is connected to a gear-box housing a bevel drive. This extensible shaft is the connecting link between projector and "Vitaphone."

Speed

By means of these two sets of gears, the speed is reduced from a motor speed of 1,200 r.p.m. to a speed on the projector driving shaft of 90 r.p.m., which corresponds to a film speed of 90 feet per minute.

The other end of the motor shaft is coupled to the turntable mechanism which is firmly attached to a heavy telescoping pedestal, the three supporting legs of which are adjustable for levelling purposes. This pedestal is separate from the motor table. A worm-gear drive is fitted in the top of the pedestal in a specially cast compartment. The worm-gear shaft is coupled to the motor shaft by a flexible coupling designed to prevent the transmission of gear noises and vibrations from the motor to the turntable. The worm gear meshes with a gear which carries the vertical shaft upon which the turntable is mounted.

Between these gears and the vertical shaft a mechanical filter or "shock absorber" is fitted consisting of a series of light springs designed to prevent the transmission of gear noises from the worm drive to the turntable and thence to record and reproducer. The gear ratio here is such that the motor shaft revs. of 1,200 p.m. is reduced so that the turntable operates at a speed of 33⅓ r.p.m., which is the correct turntable speed to synchronise with the projection speed of 90 feet per minute.

The turntable is designed to accommodate an 18-inch record, and is provided with a tension device to hold the record firmly against its surface.

Other apparatus which the projectionist has to deal with are a motor control cabinet, a fader, amplifiers with their associated units—batteries, etc., the "speakers" and their control panel.

Now without going into detail at this point concerning this equipment let us visualise what enters into the projection of a "Vitaphone" picture.

The film is threaded with the starting frame in position directly in front of the aperture, and the record placed and secured on the turntable. The reproducer needle is carefully set in the groove at the point of the starting arrow, and the motor flywheel then given a few revolutions by hand until the turntable revolves half a turn and everything is found to be working correctly.

Importance of Speed
At the right moment the motor is started up by turning a rotary snap switch on the motor control box. The matter of speed is of most importance with "Vitaphone" productions. To ensure of perfect reproduction, "Vitaphone" subjects must be projected at the same speed at which they were taken—which is exactly 90 feet per minute. If this is not strictly adhered to, the presentation is ruined for such results in causing distortion of voice or music and changes of pitch.

For running productions of the usual "silent" type, the motor speed can be regulated as desired.

The output of the reproducer goes to the fader and thence to the amplifiers. The fader is used to control the volume of the sound heard in the theatre, and to assist in controlling the sound when changing over from one projector to the other and which can be accomplished without break in the speech or music. Each record has a "fader" setting indicated on it which must be observed.

The amplifiers and associated apparatus next come into action. These amplifiers are similar in principle to those employed in the audio-frequency stages of radio sets. The output from the amplifiers goes to the loud speaker control panel from which the sound current is distributed via separate "runs" to the receivers attached to the loud speakers. Provision is made for controlling the individual loud speaker circuits and a monitoring "speaker" is installed in the projection room to enable the projectionist to follow the programme.

A dial switch is incorporated in each of the loud speaker circuits and is provided with numbered steps. This is known as a "speaker" control, and is used for "balancing" the "speakers" to get the right effect in the auditorium from the different types of subject. For this purpose three settings are used for the "speaker" controls and each record is marked A. B. or C. to indicate which of the three settings should be used. . . .

Non-Synchronous Accompaniments

The presentation of pictures for which no special synchronised accompaniments are available can be provided with an orchestral accompaniment from ordinary gramophone records. In this case, it is necessary for the exhibitor to cue the selections to be played, and records need to be changed as required during projection of film. This is termed non-synchronous reproduction. . . . To do this calls for special turntable equipment. . . .

DESIGNED BY GARY GORE
COMPOSED BY GRAPHIC COMPOSITION, INC.
ATHENS, GEORGIA
MANUFACTURED BY THE NORTH CENTRAL PUBLISHING CO.
ST. PAUL, MINNESOTA
TEXT AND DISPLAY LINES ARE SET IN PALATINO

Library of Congress Cataloging in Publication Data
Main entry under title:
The Jazz singer.
(Wisconsin/Warner Bros. screenplay series)
Includes The jazz singer, by A. A. Cohn,
screenplay of the 1927 film and
The Day of Atonement, by S. Raphaelson,
original story reprinted from Everybody's magazine, Jan. 1922.
1. The Jazz singer, [Motion picture]
2. Movingpictures, Talking—History.
I. Carringer, Robert.
II. Cohn, Alfred Abraham, 1880–1951. The jazz singer.
III. Raphaelson, Samson, 1896— The Day of Atonement.
IV. Series.
PN1997.J353J3   791.43'7   78-53295
ISBN 0-299-07660-1
ISBN 0-299-07664-4 pbk.

WW
WISCONSIN/WARNER BROS SCREENPLAY SERIES

The Wisconsin/Warner Bros. Screenplay Series, a product of the Warner Brothers Film Library, will enable film scholars, students, researchers, and aficionados to gain insights into individual American films in ways never before possible.

The Warner library was acquired in 1957 by the United Artists Corporation, which in turn donated it to the Wisconsin Center for Film and Theater Research in 1969. The massive library, housed in the State Historical Society of Wisconsin, contains eight hundred sound feature films, fifteen hundred short subjects, and nineteen thousand still negatives, as well as the legal files, press books, and screenplays of virtually every Warner film produced from 1930 until 1950. This rich treasure trove has made the University of Wisconsin one of the major centers for film research, attracting scholars from around the world. This series of published screenplays represents a creative use of the Warner library, both a boon to scholars and a tribute to United Artists.

Most published film scripts are literal transcriptions of finished films. The Wisconsin/Warner screenplays are primary source documents—the final shooting versions including revisions made during production. As such, they will explicate the art of screenwriting as film transcriptions cannot. They will help the user to understand the arts of directing and acting, as well as the other arts involved in the film-making process, in comparing these screenplays with the final films. (Films of the Warner library are available at modest rates from the United Artists nontheatrical rental library, United Artists/16 mm.)

From the eight hundred feature films in the library, the general editor and the editorial committee of the series have chosen those that have received critical recognition for their excellence of directing, screenwriting, and acting, films that are distinctive examples of their genre, those that have particular historical relevance, and some that are adaptations of well-known novels and plays. The researcher, instructor, or student can, in the judicious selection of individual volumes for close examination, gain a heightened appreciation and broad understanding of the American film and its historical role during this critical period.